FUNDAMENTALS OF CAPF PAPER 2

LEARN TO ACE UPSC CAPF AC EXAM STARTING FROM SCRATCH

V SARVESH TRIPATHI
FORMER ASSISTANT COMMANDANT, CRPF

BLUEROSE PUBLISHERS
India | U.K.

Copyright © V Sarvesh Tripathi- Former Asst Commandant , CRPF 2025

All rights reserved by author. No part of this publication may be reproduced, stored in a retrieval system or transmitted in any form or by any means, electronic, mechanical, photocopying, recording or otherwise, without the prior permission of the author. Although every precaution has been taken to verify the accuracy of the information contained herein, the publisher assumes no responsibility for any errors or omissions. No liability is assumed for damages that may result from the use of information contained within.

BlueRose Publishers takes no responsibility for any damages, losses, or liabilities that may arise from the use or misuse of the information, products, or services provided in this publication.

For permissions requests or inquiries regarding this publication,
please contact:

BLUEROSE PUBLISHERS
www.BlueRoseONE.com
info@bluerosepublishers.com
+91 8882 898 898
+4407342408967

ISBN: 978-93-7018-472-5

Cover Design: Aman Sharma
Typesetting: Pooja Sharma

First Edition: April 2025

सादर प्रणाम

मेरी लेखनी का प्रत्येक अक्षर एवं जीवन का प्रत्येक क्षण पूज्य पिताजी को समर्पित 🙏

इस पुस्तक की शुरुआत भी आप द्वारा रचित उन पंक्तियों से ही होनी चाहिए जिन्होंने सदैव मेरा मार्ग प्रशस्त किया है।

परेशानियाँ ही बढ़ाती हैं साहस

मुसीबत से मिलती है मंजिल सुहानी

जो चंदन है शीतल झुलसते बदन को

बहुत मीठा लगता मरुस्थल में पानी

- स्व॰ गंगाशरण राम त्रिपाठी

पूर्व न्यायाधीश

For my wife Noopur, my greatest inspiration, my support system and my truest friend who almost forced me to write this book.

(forced me to write this acknowledgement as well ;)

Preface

The Union Public Service Commission (UPSC) conducts the Central Armed Police Forces (CAPF) Assistant Commandant (AC) examination to recruit dynamic and dedicated officers for India's Central Armed Police Forces . It is a very beautifully crafted paper having three stages. Paper-2 which focuses on General Studies, Essay, and Comprehension, plays a crucial role in evaluating a candidate's analytical ability, writing skills, and command over language.

This book has been meticulously designed to cater to the specific demands of UPSC CAPF Paper 2 with my understanding and experience over it, ensuring a structured approach to essay writing, arguments, precis, comprehension, and effective communication. It provides a comprehensive collection of essays on contemporary issues, model reports, precise summaries, and grammar exercises, all tailored to meet the exam's requirements.

Each chapter follows a systematic approach—starting with conceptual clarity, followed by examples, practice exercises, and model answers.

Whether you are a first-time aspirant or a seasoned candidate, this book aims to be your trusted companion in mastering Paper 2. It will not only enhance your writing skills but also develop a structured thought process essential for success in the examination.

This book is a tribute to my guiding light my father Late Shri G S R Tripathi Retired Judge from Bihar judicial Service and result of constant support and motivation by my wife Smt Noopur Tripathi (IRAS) and and very important insights by My Elder brother Shri S Devesh Tripathi Deputy Commandant CISF (AIR- 27 , UPSC 2012).

We hope this book serves as a valuable resource in your UPSC CAPF journey and helps you achieve your goal of serving the nation with dedication and integrity.

Best wishes!

V S Tripathi

27-03-2025

हिंदी माध्यम के अभ्यर्थियों के लिए संदेश

प्रिय अभ्यर्थियों

अपने अनुभव और इस परीक्षा के परिणामों के आधार पर मैं बिल्कुल साफ़ करना चाहता हूँ की ये परीक्षा अंग्रेजी के ज्ञान की परीक्षा बिल्कुल नहीं है। अगर आप सामान्य अंग्रेजी व्याकरण से परिचित हैं और हिंदी निबंध पर आपकी पकड़ अच्छी है तो आपकी सफ़लता निश्चित है।

निबंध आपको 80 अंकों में ज़्यादा से ज़्यादा अंक अर्जित करने का अवसर देते हैं और उसके बाद बचे हुए सारे भागों में अगर आपने सामान्य प्रदर्शन बुद्धिमत्ता के साथ किया तो आप आसानी से 100 के जादुई आंकड़े के पास पहुँच सकते जो आपकी अकादमी तक की राह प्रशस्त करेगा।

ध्यान रखें की इस प्रतिस्पर्धा में सामान्य अंग्रेजी समझना, लिखना व बोल पाना अति आवश्यक है और उसका कोई विकल्प नहीं किंतु इससे तनिक भी हतोत्साहित न हों, आज से अभी से अंग्रेजी व्याकरण पर मेहनत शुरू करें और निरंतर प्रयास करते रहें। साथ ही साथ हिंदी निबंध को इतना धारदार बना लें की वो 80 अंकों में ही आपको इतने अंक दिला पाएं की बाक़ी भागों की त्रुटियां नगण्य हो जाएँ।

मैं अनगिनत ऐसे सफल अभ्यर्थियों को जानता हूँ जिन्होंने हिंदी माध्यम से सफलता प्राप्त की और आज वरिष्ठ अधिकारी हैं।

आपको बस अपनी तैयारी में ईमानदार रहना है और बिना किसी नकारात्मक विचार के मेहनत करते रहना है। पेपर 1 के लिए अगर समुचित तैयारी की जाए तो वही तथ्य आपके इस पेपर में काम आएंगे और अलग से तथ्यों या किसी सामग्री की आवश्यकता नहीं होगी, पिछले वर्षों के प्रश्नों से सीख ले सकते हैं किंतु उनको रटने की गलती ना करें क्यूंकि लिखना आपको ख़ुद होगा तभी अच्छे अंक मिलेंगे।

तो बस ख़ुद की तैयारी और बड़ों के आशीर्वचनों पर विश्वास करें और लग जाएँ तैयारी में क्यूँकि आपके और सफलता में बस एक ईमानदार प्रयास की दूरी है अब।

रात जितनी ही संगीन होगी

सुबह उतनी ही रंगीन होगी

ग़म ना कर गर है बादल घनेरा

किसके रोके रुका है सवेरा ॥

- साहिर लुधियानवी

About the Author

V. Sarvesh Tripathi cleared UPSC CAPF in 2013, first attempt straight out of college with obtaining more than 100 marks in paper 2. He has worked eight years as assistant commandant in CRPF on various postings ranging from Gadchiroli to Kashmir and has been decorated with numerous commendations and medals.

He did his graduation in BTech bioinformatics, got selected in his fourth year. Continuing his academic pursuit, he did MA (history), MBA, post graduate diploma in disaster management and LLB. He also has a diploma in IPR, trademarks, Patents and copyright.

Shri VS Tripathi is also the managing director of Gyansthali Academy and Adamya classes, Gorakhpur, Uttar Pradesh.

He has mentored many students at various coaching institutes for UPSC civil services and UPSC CAPF.

Contents

Paper 2 1

Essay 5

Arguments 16

Precis Writing 20

Report Writing 30

Reading Comprehension 35

Grammar 43

Nouns 44

Pronouns 46

Verbs 49

Prepositions 53

Conjunction 56

Direct/Indirect 69

Articles 75

Gerunds and Infinitives 80

Modal Verbs 90

Sample Papers 94

Paper 2

UPSC CAPF AC Paper 2 is a descriptive test focusing on General Studies, Essay, and Comprehension, requiring candidates to answer in English or Hindi, with a minimum qualifying score of 50 out of 200 marks.

Here's a more detailed breakdown:

- **Nature of the Paper:** Paper 2 is a descriptive examination. Paper II includes topics such as Comprehension, Essay Writing, Precis Writing, Counter Argument, and Communication skills.
- **Syllabus:** The syllabus includes General Studies, Essay, and Comprehension.
- **Language:** Candidates can choose to answer in either English or Hindi.
- **Marks:** The total marks for Paper 2 are 200, and candidates need to secure a minimum qualifying exam which can vary .

Format: Paper 2 consists of following indicative format

4 essays of maximum 300 words = 80 marks (20X4)

2 arguments = 40 marks (20X2)

2 reports of maximum 200 words = 20 marks (10X2)

One Precis = 15 marks

Reading comprehension for one passage = 20 marks

Grammar and vocabulary = 25 marks

In this book we will be discussing each of the above questions in detail along with practice questions. Paper 2 requires regular writing practice along with factual knowledge. We will discuss the correct formats and practices to write on the above topics.

Material for Paper 2

The most common question i come across is where to get materials for paper 2 so here i want to clear the air once and for all .

There is no extra material for paper 2 per se and don't worry about it at all , you just have to study properly for your paper 1 and that is it . Everything you read and learn for paper 1 is material for paper 2, all the facts and logic you learn there will be used here .

Current affairs you read for paper 1 and that won't change for paper 2 as well . So you just need to study religiously for paper 1 and then try to use every relevant fact in paper 2 while writing . Make notes for different sections separately for paper 2 like science and tech , polity , significant personalities, current affairs etc and you are done for paper 2 .

So basically paper 2 is your complete paper 1 + your writing skills and a bit of English grammar.

Get in straight in your mind and give your best shot guys .

All the best !

Understanding the soul of paper 2:

In my opinion, In all the exams conducted by UPSC across the country, the paper two in UPSC CAPF, is the most beautifully crafted test paper which carves out your knowledge of general studies, English and your presentation skills. Therefore, you have to understand the basic theme of the paper before starting it. In all the three stages of the examination paper two is one stage you can bank upon properly. It will never disappoint or cheat you.

Suppose you prepared very well for paper one and the specific topics or subjects that you prepared very efficiently, had very little portion in the paper that year. There is no fixed frame for paper 1 and UPSC is well known for leaving out some topics entirely from the paper.

As for the interview part of UPSC, everyone knows it is full of surprises and can go any which way. This leaves paper 2 of UPSC CAPF to be the most dependable paper.

The most important part of paper two is completing all the questions within the given timeframe. It has been seen that many bright and well prepared Students failed in the exam simply because they failed to attempt all the questions. Attempting all the questions within the given time frame and word limit ensures good marks. This can only be achieved by a lot of practice.

First and the most important part of paper two is completing the paper in the timeframe given without leaving any question and when I say this, this statement is based upon the experiences of my students who were very very bright and very much prepared for the paper failed in the exam, just because they could not complete the paper two. Second is understanding the evaluator's perspective because it is a human mind which is evaluating your copy and your copy is there to represent you, nothing else. So every line you write should be written with a new perspective embedded in it.

Introduction part of every topic is very vital because it would be the first thing your evaluator will see. Based upon your introduction only, the evaluator can make an opinion of your skills

This test is not an evaluation of literature or very refined English. Even an aspirant having a basic knowledge of English can clear this exam easily. You have to understand that the medium of the exam is basically English, including the fact that you can write your essay in Hindi, which makes you call it, Hindi medium, but the whole process in general is in English medium, including the interview part of it.

Because the day you become an assistant commandant, you have to deal with people of every linguistic community, and in that case English will be your best saviour. You don't have to be very literary or equipped with very decorative English because that would make the paper tough to understand for the evaluator. In some cases being very clear and basic in your writing will eventually fetch you good marks. On the other hand, you don't need to be scare If you are not very good at English. You just have to communicate in basic English. Write short sentences and your task is done.

How to choose the topics for essay:

Before we start discussing the format of the essay, let us discuss the first step, which is choosing the 4 essays out of the six given options.

It is the most important step while writing paper 2. First, analyse all the topics and then decide on the basis of your own strength and writing skills. You should choose your topics according to the depth of facts you have and your understanding over the topic. When you have enough facts and understanding over the topic, the time taken in completing the essay would be less.

Suppose if you are a science student, you should avoid philosophical topics and go with the scientific topics since it would fetch you good marks in lesser time. And if you are good with your writing skills with respect to philosophy topics, you should go with the philosophy topics. Be careful not to overdo it and devote more time which may hamper the other topics in the paper.

Essay

Essay is one of the most important parts of paper 2 since it carries 80 marks out of 200. Given the weightage it carries, it is very important to follow its format while delivering your best effort. Essay must be done in three parts, the introduction, the body and the conclusion.

Introduction (Around 60 words): Introduction is the first part that an evaluator sees. It is important to write a good introduction. Introduction itself has three parts. First is introducing the topic The second is as to why it is important. That can be explained by connecting it to some recent event. Next is to connect it to the main body of the essay by providing a brief overview of what you will discuss

Body Paragraphs (2-3 paragraphs, around 100 words each): Body of an essay is used for elaborating the topic with facts. This is where you write down all the facts and information regarding the topic. Provide evidence, examples, or arguments to support your point. Use transitions to smoothly connect your ideas between paragraphs.

Conclusion (Around 50 words): Conclude your essay while summarising the main points discussed in the essay. State your thesis or main argument. This is where you give your view regarding the theme of the essay. Be careful to give a balanced, uncontroversial view while refraining from criticising the Government or the judiciary. You can end the essay with a thought-provoking statement or a call to action.

Here's a sample structure for a 300-word essay on the following topics of climate change:

Introduction (60 words): Climate change refers to long-term change in the average weather patterns that have come to define Earth's local, regional and global climates. The India AI Mission and Gates Foundation will be soon signing an Memorandum of Understanding (MoU) to revolutionise agriculture, healthcare, education, and climate change initiatives. With rising global temperatures and extreme weather events becoming more frequent, it is crucial to explore the causes and potential solutions to mitigate its impact.

Body Paragraph 1 (100 words): One of the primary causes of climate change is the emission of greenhouse gases, such as carbon dioxide and methane, primarily from human activities such as burning fossil fuels and deforestation. These gases trap heat in the Earth's atmosphere, leading to a rise in temperatures.

Body Paragraph 2 (100 words): The consequences of climate change are wide-ranging and severe, affecting ecosystems, weather patterns, and human societies. Increased temperatures contribute to the melting of polar ice caps, rising sea levels, and more frequent and intense natural disasters, displacing communities and threatening biodiversity.

Conclusion (50 words): In conclusion, addressing climate change requires concerted efforts at both individual and collective levels. By transitioning to renewable energy sources, adopting sustainable practices, and advocating for policy changes, we can work towards mitigating the effects of climate change and building a more resilient future for generations to come.

Points to keep in mind while writing the essay

a. Keep the sentences short. Use full stops often.
b. Use simple language. Avoid jargon.
c. Avoid grammatical mistakes.
d. Do not exceed the word limit.
e. Follow the structure.
f. Do not ignore the introduction or conclusion.
g. Do not give wrong factual information.
h. Do not give controversial opinions.
i. Stick to the topic. Avoid digressing away from the theme of the essay

Some more sample essays are as follows

A. Is India's mixed economy model the most effective path for economic growth?

Is India's Mixed Economy Model the Most Effective Path for Economic Growth?

A mixed economy, integrates both capitalist and socialist principles. This model allows for a balance between government intervention and private enterprise, ensuring both economic growth and social welfare. Since independence, India has relied on state-led initiatives for infrastructure and essential industries while allowing private businesses to drive innovation and efficiency.

One of the key advantages of this model is its ability to promote balanced development. The government's involvement in crucial sectors such as healthcare, education, and infrastructure ensures equitable distribution of resources. At the same time, private sector participation fuels investment, employment, and technological advancement. This combination has helped India achieve significant economic progress while safeguarding social stability.

However, the mixed economy model is not without its challenges. Bureaucratic inefficiencies and excessive regulation often slow down economic progress and create hurdles for private enterprises. Additionally, while sectors like technology and services have flourished, others such as agriculture and small-scale industries continue to struggle due to inconsistent policies and lack of modernization. Furthermore, many public sector enterprises operate inefficiently and depend heavily on government subsidies, creating a fiscal burden.

Despite these challenges, the mixed economy model remains relevant. With continuous reforms, such as reducing bureaucratic red tape and encouraging private investment in key sectors, India can enhance economic growth while ensuring inclusive development. A flexible and evolving approach will allow the country to harness the strengths of both the public and private sectors. By addressing inefficiencies and adapting to changing global trends, India's mixed economy can remain an effective path for sustainable economic progress.

B. "Constitutional amendments in India: Balancing stability with the need for change."

Constitutional Amendments in India: Balancing Stability with the Need for Change

Constitutional amendments are formal changes to a country's constitution, reflecting societal shifts or the need to address pressing issues, and typically require a rigorous process of proposal, debate, and approval. Recently the constitutional amendment regarding delimitation is in the news. The Indian Constitution, adopted in 1950, is a living document that reflects the aspirations of a diverse and evolving society. To maintain its relevance, the Constitution provides for amendments, ensuring a balance between stability and necessary change. This amendment process, outlined in Article

368, allows for modifications while safeguarding the core principles of democracy, fundamental rights, and federalism.

The framers of the Constitution envisioned a dynamic governance structure, where amendments would enable adaptation to societal and political transformations. Since independence, over a hundred amendments have been enacted, addressing socio-economic progress, political restructuring, and judicial interpretations. Some landmark amendments include the First Amendment (1951), which imposed reasonable restrictions on free speech; the 42nd Amendment (1976), which sought to strengthen central authority during the Emergency; and the 73rd and 74th Amendments (1992), which empowered local governance institutions.

However, the amendment process is designed to ensure that changes are not arbitrary. The Constitution distinguishes between simple and rigid amendments, requiring either a simple majority in Parliament or a more rigorous procedure, including state ratification, for significant changes. This dual approach prevents impulsive alterations while permitting essential reforms.

Despite its flexibility, constitutional amendments have sparked debates on judicial review and the basic structure doctrine. In the Kesavananda Bharati case (1973), the Supreme Court ruled that Parliament cannot alter the Constitution's fundamental framework, ensuring that amendments do not erode democratic and secular foundations.

Balancing stability with change remains a challenge. While amendments have facilitated progress, concerns about political misuse persist. Therefore, any constitutional change must be approached with caution, maintaining democratic integrity while addressing contemporary needs. The Indian Constitution continues to evolve, reflecting the aspirations of its people while upholding its foundational ethos.

C. Role of Indian Startups in Driving Technological Innovation and Entrepreneurship

India has emerged as a global hub for startups, fostering technological innovation and entrepreneurship. With a vibrant ecosystem supported by government initiatives, venture capital investments, and a growing talent pool, Indian startups are revolutionizing various sectors, including fintech, healthtech, edtech, and e-commerce. These startups are not only contributing to economic growth but also addressing societal challenges through innovative solutions.

One of the key drivers of this startup boom is the government's proactive approach, exemplified by initiatives like Startup India, Digital India, and Atmanirbhar Bharat. These programs provide financial incentives, tax benefits, and regulatory ease, encouraging young entrepreneurs to take risks and develop groundbreaking technologies. Additionally, the rise of incubators, accelerators, and co-working spaces has nurtured innovation by offering mentorship and funding opportunities.

Indian startups have played a crucial role in technological advancements. Companies like Flipkart, Paytm, and BYJU'S have transformed e-commerce, digital payments, and education, respectively. Similarly, deep-tech startups focusing on artificial intelligence, blockchain, and biotechnology are positioning India as a leader in emerging technologies. The rise of unicorns—startups valued at over a billion dollars—further reflects the success and potential of India's entrepreneurial ecosystem.

Furthermore, startups are generating employment and empowering local communities by bridging urban-rural divides through digital access. Agri-tech startups, for instance, are using AI and IoT to optimize farming practices, improving productivity and sustainability.

Despite challenges like regulatory complexities, funding constraints, and global competition, Indian startups continue to innovate and expand internationally. With sustained government support and increased investments in research and development, India is poised to become a global leader in technology-driven entrepreneurship. The startup revolution is not just shaping the economy but also inspiring a culture of innovation across the nation

Following are some practice topics for essay

A Economics

1. "Privatization vs. nationalization: Which approach is better for India's economic development?"

2. "The role of government intervention in shaping India's economic system."

3. "Sustainable development vs. rapid industrialization: Balancing economic growth with environmental concerns in India."

5. "The impact of economic reforms and liberalization on India's economy."

6. "Income inequality in India: Addressing disparities within the economic system."

7. "The role of small and medium enterprises (SMEs) in driving India's economic growth."

8. "Challenges and opportunities for foreign investment in India's economy."

9. "Digital transformation: How technology is reshaping India's economic landscape."

10. "The informal economy in India: Assessing its significance and challenges."

B Polity

1. "Federalism in India: Striking a balance between centralization and state autonomy."

2. "The effectiveness of India's parliamentary system compared to other forms of government."

3. "Electoral reforms in India: Enhancing democracy and political representation."

4. "Secularism vs. communalism: Upholding India's secular fabric in a diverse society."

5. "Judicial activism in India: Strengthening democracy or undermining separation of powers?"

6. "Reservation policies in India: Addressing social justice or perpetuating inequality?"

7. "Women's political representation in India: Breaking barriers or facing systemic challenges?"

8. "The role of regional political parties in shaping India's national politics."

9. "Election funding and political corruption: Combating corruption in India's polity."

C Science and Technology

1. "India's space program: A testament to technological prowess or misplaced priorities?"

2. "Digital India initiative: Empowering citizens or widening the digital divide?"

3. "BharatNet project: Bridging the rural-urban digital gap or facing implementation challenges?"

4. "."

5. "Impact of artificial intelligence and machine learning on India's technological landscape."

6. "5G rollout in India: Opportunities, challenges, and implications for the economy."

7. "Biotechnology advancements in India: Revolutionizing healthcare

8. "Renewable energy technologies: India's progress towards a sustainable future."

9. "Cybersecurity challenges in India: Safeguarding digital infrastructure and privacy."

10. "Smart cities mission: Transforming urban spaces with technology

D Environment

1. "India's role in global climate change negotiations: Leader or laggard?"

2. "Air pollution crisis in Indian cities: Urgent measures vs. economic considerations."

3. "Water scarcity in India: Balancing agricultural needs, urban demands, and environmental conservation."

4. "Impact of deforestation on India's biodiversity and climate resilience."

5. "Renewable energy transition in India: Progress, challenges, and future prospects."

6. "Urbanization and its environmental consequences in India: Mitigating pollution and habitat loss."

7. "The role of traditional knowledge and practices in mitigating climate change in India."

8. "Climate refugees in India: Addressing the challenges of displacement and resettlement."

9. "Plastic pollution: Strategies for reducing single-use plastics in India."

10. "Economic development vs. environmental conservation: Striking a balance in India's policy approach."

E Indian history

1. "The legacy of colonialism in India: Economic exploitation, cultural impact, and lingering effects."

2. "Cultural pluralism in India: Celebrating diversity or facing challenges of communalism?"

3. "The significance of ancient Indian civilization: Contributions to world culture, science, and philosophy."

4. "Partition of India: Understanding the historical context, legacy, and implications for modern-day India and Pakistan."

5. "The role of women in Indian history: From ancient times to contemporary struggles for equality."

6. "Caste system in India: Historical roots, contemporary relevance, and challenges to social justice."

7. "The impact of the Indian independence movement: Lessons learned and ongoing struggles for social and economic justice."

8. "Indian literature and arts: Exploring the richness and diversity of literary traditions, visual arts, and performing arts."

9. "Religious pluralism in India: Coexistence, conflict, and the quest for religious harmony."

10. "Indian diaspora: Contributions to global culture, economy, and diplomacy."

F internal security

a. **Counter-terrorism Strategies**:

1. India should prioritize intelligence-led counter-terrorism measures over military interventions.

2. There is a need for stronger international cooperation in combating terrorism within India's borders.

3. Socio-economic development programs in conflict-affected areas are more effective in countering terrorism than purely military approaches.

b. Insurgency and Naxalism

1. The government can effectively address the root causes of Naxalism by implementing comprehensive socio-economic development programs.

2. The government should pursue dialogue and reconciliation with insurgent groups alongside military operations to address the root causes of insurgency.

3. Corruption within security forces contributes significantly to the perpetuation of insurgency movements.

c. **Border Security**:

1. Building physical barriers along India's borders is an effective strategy to enhance security, complemented by technological solutions.

2. India should manage its border disputes with China through diplomatic negotiations and adherence to international law to ensure security and stability.

3. Regional alliances and international organizations play a significant role in bolstering India's border security

d. **Cybersecurity**:

1. Is India adequately prepared to defend against cyber threats, including state-sponsored cyber-attacks and cyber-terrorism?

2. Should the government prioritize legislation for cybersecurity, even if it potentially infringes on individual privacy rights?

3. How can India bridge the digital divide to ensure cybersecurity measures benefit all segments of society?

e. **Communal and Ethnic Violence**:

1. Stricter laws should be implemented to combat hate speech and prevent the incitement of violence on social media platforms.

2. Addressing historical grievances and inequalities is essential to prevent recurring cycles of violence.

f. **Internal Displacement and Refugee Crisis**:

1. India should adopt more inclusive policies to integrate refugees into mainstream society

2. Civil society organizations and international humanitarian agencies play a crucial role in supporting India's response to internal displacement and refugee crises

g. **Police Reforms**:

1. Is there a need for comprehensive reforms within India's police forces

2. decentralising the policing powers will improve law enforcement at the grassroots level

3. police-community relations need to be strengthened for maintaining internal security?

G Philosophical topics

a. Meaning of life:

1. The pursuit of personal fulfillment is the primary purpose of life.

2. The meaning of life lies in the pursuit of knowledge and understanding.

3. Love and connection with others constitute the essence of life's meaning.

4. The meaning of life is to leave a lasting impact or legacy on the world.

5. Spiritual or religious beliefs provide the most compelling explanation for the meaning of life.

6. Life's meaning is derived from embracing and transcending adversity and suffering.

7. The pursuit of happiness and joy is the fundamental purpose of existence.

8. Life's meaning is found in the pursuit of self-discovery and personal growth.

9. The meaning of life is to find and fulfill one's unique purpose or calling.

10. The pursuit of balance and harmony in all aspects of life is the key to finding meaning.

b. Leadership

1. The Role of Emotional Intelligence in Effective Leadership.

5. The Importance of Visionary Leadership in Driving Organizational Success.

6.8. The Impact of Inclusive Leadership on Team Performance and Engagement.

c. Motivation

1. The Role of Intrinsic versus Extrinsic Motivation in Achieving Goals.

2. The Power of Goal Setting: How Clear Objectives Drive Motivation.

3. Understanding the Impact of Positive Reinforcement on Motivation.

4. Overcoming Procrastination: Strategies for Boosting Motivation.

5. The Influence of Self-Efficacy on Motivation and Performance.

6. The Role of Autonomy in Fostering Motivation and Engagement.

7. Motivation in the Workplace: Creating a Culture of Recognition and Appreciation.

8. The Impact of Mindset on Motivation: Fixed vs. Growth Mindset.

9. Motivation and Mental Health: Strategies for Maintaining Motivation During Challenging Times.

10. The Connection Between Passion and Motivation: Pursuing What Truly Drives You.

Arguments

Argument is the most important section of paper two from the aspirant's perspective, as it is written in a point wise manner and it fetches good marks. The best thing about it is that it takes very less time which gives you more time to devote to the essay. An ideal argument carries three parts:

<u>Introduction</u>: introduction should be very short. It is only meant to introduce the topic and open the discussion. It should not exceed more than 3 to 4 lines.

<u>For and Against the statement</u>: for and against that statement should be done in 4 to 5 points. Each point should start with a subheading. Each point should be explained in brief with examples, illustrations and supporting facts. An argument carries 20 marks so it should be written in around 200 words.

<u>Conclusion</u>: the conclusion in an argument should be very balanced. It should be of the same length as the introduction. It Should summarise your arguments in maximum 3 to 4 lines. It should be neutral and not reflect any kind of bias.

Example:

Topic: Pros and Cons of Online Learning

Introduction:

- Brief overview of online learning

- Thesis statement: While online learning offers convenience and flexibility, it also presents challenges such as lack of face-to-face interaction and potential distractions.

Body Paragraphs:

1. **Pros (Positive Aspects):**

- Convenience: Access to education from anywhere with an internet connection.

- Flexibility: Ability to study at one's own pace and schedule.

- Variety of courses: Wide range of subjects and programs available online.

2. **Cons (Negative Aspects):**

- Lack of face-to-face interaction: Reduced opportunities for discussion and collaboration.

- Potential for distractions: Difficulty staying focused without a structured learning environment.

- Limited access to resources: Some online courses may lack access to hands-on materials or specialized equipment.

Conclusion:

- Recap of pros and cons discussed.

- Reiteration of thesis.

- Final thoughts: While online learning has its benefits, it's essential to consider both its advantages and drawbacks when deciding on the most suitable educational approach.

Practice Topics for Arguments

1. "Social media platforms should be held legally responsible for the spread of misinformation."
2. "Universal Basic Income is a viable solution to combat poverty in developed countries."
3. "Climate change should be treated as a national security threat by governments worldwide."
4. "The use of facial recognition technology by governments should be heavily regulated."
5. "Remote work should become the default for all eligible employees even after the pandemic."
6. "The wealth gap is a more pressing issue than the income gap in modern societies."
7. "All countries should prioritize renewable energy sources over fossil fuels."
8. "Governments should implement a tax on wealth rather than just income."
9. "The use of genetically modified organisms (GMOs) in agriculture is necessary for global food security."

10. "Space exploration should be primarily funded by private companies rather than governments."
11. "The United Nations should have more authority to intervene in conflicts between nations."
12. "Free speech should have limitations on social media platforms to prevent hate speech and misinformation."
13. "Cryptocurrencies should be regulated by governments to prevent illegal activities."
14. "Governments should prioritize investment in public transportation over expanding road networks."
15. "The use of drones for military purposes should be heavily restricted."

These topics cover a range of current affairs and offer ample scope for debate and discussion.

Here are some topics for arguments on current affairs in India:

1. "The implementation of the Citizenship Amendment Act (CAA) will have positive effects on India's refugee policy."
2. "Reservation in educational institutions and government jobs should be based solely on economic criteria rather than caste."
3. "The government's handling of the COVID-19 pandemic in India has been effective."
4. "The recent farm laws introduced by the Indian government will benefit farmers in the long term."
5. "India's space program is a valuable investment despite economic challenges."
6. "The rise of Hindu nationalism poses a threat to India's secular fabric."
7. "The One Nation One Election proposal is a feasible solution to India's electoral challenges."
8. "The privatization of Air India is essential for its survival and competitiveness."
9. "India's approach to dealing with neighboring countries like Pakistan and China is appropriate."

10. "The New Education Policy (NEP) will bring about significant positive changes in India's education system."
11. "The digital divide in India is widening and requires urgent government intervention."
12. "India's stance on climate change is inadequate considering its global impact."
13. "The criminalization of triple talaq is a step forward for women's rights in India."
14. "India's judicial system needs significant reforms to ensure timely justice delivery."
15. "The recent electoral reforms introduced by the Election Commission of India will enhance the democratic process."

Precis Writing

Writing a good précis involves summarizing a text's main points concisely and accurately while maintaining its essence and tone.

Here's a step-by-step guide:

- Read the original text carefully to understand its main ideas, arguments, and supporting details.
- Identify the text's thesis or central argument and the key points that support it.
- Determine the text's tone, style, and intended audience.
- Write a single sentence that captures the author's main argument or thesis.
- Craft a concise summary by including only the essential points that support the main argument.
- Eliminate any unnecessary details, examples, or repetitions.
- Ensure coherence and logical flow between sentences while maintaining the original text's structure.
- Use your own words to paraphrase the original text, avoiding direct quotations.
- Aim for clarity, precision, and brevity in your writing.
- Revise and edit your précis to ensure accuracy, coherence, and adherence to the word limit (usually one-third to one-fourth of the original text's length).
- Finally, check for grammar, spelling, and punctuation errors before finalizing your précis.

Practice paragraphs for précis:

A. When Amartya Sen titles a book The Argumentative Indian, the reader naturally assumes something by way of an autobiography. (Or, as a friend teased, perhaps it was about me.) The joke is no doubt intentional, but Sen's goal is something much grander. As many Indians have watched in horror, over the past decade the term "secular" has successfully turned into a curse in Indian politics. It is this taboo that Sen tries to combat, by demonstrating two things: that Indian culture is richer than only Hindu culture, and that Indian culture—*including* Hindu culture—has a long and rich *argumentative* tradition. For Sen believes that where argument lives, scepticism thrives, and fundamentalism must inevitably fail.

First, the goal of Sen's project. It would seem difficult for just about anyone who was raised in a traditional Indian Hindu environment to reconcile the oxymoronic notion of "fundamentalist Hinduism"; Sen's goal here is to expose this line of thought, explaining precisely what it is about Hinduism that makes fundamentalism meaningless. The openness of faith Sen was exposed to led him to a muscularly, militantly secular bent of mind. Borrowing a leaf from a "Jewish atheist" I know, I would regard Sen as a "cultural Hindu". All these descriptions apply equally well to me, so it is a project I desperately wish to succeed.

There is the goal, and then there is its execution. Here, Sen falls disturbingly flat. He retreads the same tiny arguments repeatedly—a quote from the Rig Veda here, an excerpt from the Ramayana there—driving the reader first to frustration and then to outright concern. Is this the best we can do as an argument? Was Sen simply lazy, or is the evidence really that thin on the ground? His euphoric embrace of Ashoka and Akbar are bound to mislead a Western reader who is unlikely to realise that they were significant outliers to an at least tepid, and sometimes disturbing, mean. It is, ultimately, a very unfulfilling, and therefore worrying, fare.

The book's other major undoing is its format. This is a collection of essays from over a decade, which have since been annotated by Sen. His scholarly touch in this process is evident: the number of forward and backward references, and the substantial indices, demonstrate that this was no mere stapling together of pages. But that superficial thoroughness cannot mask a deep problem: there is something embarrassing about seeing effectively the same essay rewritten about eight different times in slightly different contexts, and the degree of repetition of a small number of facts could be used as a counter-argument by his foes who would argue that it lays bare how thin his argument is.

These essays constitute the first two quarters: Voice and Heterodoxy, and Culture and Communication. The book is somewhat rescued by the second half: Politics and Protest, and Reason and Identity. Here Sen comes alive as the great social economist he is, walking an interesting line between free-trader and social conscience. When, late in the book, he discusses the controversial phenomenon of the "million missing women"—the victims of society's treatment of girls and women—and you then realize *he coined the theory, you wonder if perhaps economists, like all other experts, should always consider sticking to what they do best—even if their goals in straying are truly noble.*

Précis:

In *The Argumentative Indian*, Amartya Sen seeks to defend Indian secularism and argue against the rise of fundamentalism, emphasizing India's rich tradition of argument and skepticism, which he believes can combat intolerance. Sen's goal is to show that Indian culture, including Hinduism, is diverse and that fundamentalism has no grounding in the open nature of Hindu philosophy. However, the execution of his argument is disappointing. Sen repeats small arguments from sources like the Rig Veda and Ramayana, offering little new insight, which frustrates the reader. His focus on historical figures like Ashoka and Akbar misleads the reader about the broader, often less tolerant, history of India. Additionally, the book's format, a collection of essays, leads to excessive repetition, which weakens the overall argument. The latter half of the book, which delves into topics like politics and social issues, is more engaging, especially when Sen addresses the issue of missing women. Despite its flaws, the book highlights the importance of skepticism in combating fundamentalism, even if its scholarly execution falls short.

B. From freedom at midnight

It was the winter of a great nation's discontent. An air of melancholia hung like a chill fog over London. Rarely, if ever, had Britain's capital ushered in a New Year in a mood so bleak, so morose. Hardly a home in the city that festive morning could furnish enough hot water to allow a man to shave or a woman to cover the bottom of her washbasin. Londoners had greeted the New Year in bedrooms so cold their breath had drifted in the air like puffs of smoke. Precious few of them had greeted it with a hangover. Whisky, in the places where it had been available the night before for New Year's Eve celebrations, had cost £8 a bottle. The streets were almost deserted. The passers-by hurrying down their pavements were grim, joyless creatures, threadbare in old uniforms or clothes barely holding together after eight years of make-do and mend. What few cars there were darted about like fugitive phantoms guiltily consuming Britain's rare and rationed petrol. A special stench, the odour of post-war London, permeated the streets. It was the rancid smell of charred ruins drifting up like an autumn mist from thousands of bombed-out buildings. And yet, that sad, joyless city was the capital of a conquering nation. Only seventeen months before, the British had emerged victorious from mankind's most terrible conflict. Their achievements, their courage in adversity then, had inspired an admiration such as the world had never before accorded them. The cost of their victory, however, had almost vanquished the British. Britain's industry was crippled, her exchequer bankrupt, her once haughty pound sterling surviving only on injections of American and Canadian dollars, her treasury unable to pay the staggering debt she'd run up to finance the war. Foundries and factories were closing everywhere. Over two million Britons were unemployed. Coal production was lower than it had been a decade earlier and, as a result, every day, some part of Britain was without electric power for hours. For Londoners, the New Year beginning would be the eighth consecutive year they'd lived under severe rationing of almost every product they consumed: food, fuel, drinks, energy, shoes, clothing. 'Starve and shiver' had become the byword of a people who'd defeated Hitler proclaiming 'V for Victory' and 'Thumbs Up'.

Certainly! Here's a précis that is approximately one-third the length of the original passage:

Précis:

In the bleak winter following World War II, London ushered in the New Year with a sense of deep gloom. Homes lacked basic comforts like hot water, streets were deserted, and people appeared worn and joyless, enduring cold, rationing, and poverty. Despite recent victory in the war, Britain was economically devastated—its industries failing, its currency dependent on foreign aid, and millions unemployed. Daily life was marked by power cuts and shortages of essentials. The once-proud victors now lived under the shadow of hardship, with "starve and shiver" replacing the triumphant slogans of the past.

C

It was malaria back then; I'd been infected a couple of weeks prior by an East African mosquito in a tent outside of the Serengeti and fell sick once we were home again. I was admitted to Hudiksvall Hospital and nobody could understand why all my results were off the charts; when at last they gave me the diagnosis, the doctors lined up to get a look at the woman with the exotic affliction. A fire blazed behind my brow, and I woke at dawn every morning at the hospital from the sound of my own breathing and a headache unlike anything I'd ever experienced before. Following our trip to Tanzania, I'd gone straight to Hälsingland to visit my grandfather on his deathbed. Instead I fell ill and nearly died myself. I spent more than a week at the hospital, but by the time Johanna gave me this novel, I was curled up in our bedroom in Hägersten, where they had taken me by ambulance via a liver biopsy in Uppsala. I don't remember the results – there's not much I can recall from that summer – but I'll never forget our apartment, the book, or her. The novel disappeared inside the fever and headache, fused with them, and somewhere in that mix is the line that runs all the way to today, a vein of emotion electrified by illness and fear, which is what propels me to the bookcase this afternoon to find that specific novel. Ruthless fever and headache, fretful thoughts crowding behind the eyes, the whooshing of impending distress: I recognise it all because I've experienced it before – the boxes of useless painkillers on the floor by the bed, the bottles of sparkling water I guzzle without any reprieve to my thirst. The images start rolling the instant I shut my eyes: horses' hooves in a dry desert, dank basements full of mute ghosts, big vowels screaming at me – it's the full standard menu of nightmares I've had since I was a small child, only with the added sprinkling of death and annihilation that is the territory of illness.

The author recounts a severe bout of malaria contracted in East Africa, which manifested upon returning home, leading to hospitalization in Hudiksvall. Doctors were baffled by the extreme test results until the diagnosis was confirmed, drawing fascination due to its rarity. Enduring relentless fever, headaches, and disorienting illness, the author's memories of that summer remain fragmented, except for the presence of a novel given by Johanna. The book became intertwined with the suffering, forming a lasting emotional thread that resurfaces years later when illness strikes again. As distressing symptoms return, they evoke past nightmares and fears, reinforcing the connection between sickness, memory, and literature.

Practice paragraphs for precis

D from when things fall apart

Sometimes we feel guilty, sometimes arrogant. Sometimes our thoughts and memories terrify us and make us feel totally miserable. Thoughts go through our minds all the time, and when we sit, we are providing a lot of space for all of them to arise. Like clouds in a big sky or waves in a vast sea, all our thoughts are given the space to appear. If one hangs on and sweeps us away, whether we call it pleasant or unpleasant, the instruction is to label it all "thinking" with as much openness and kindness as we can muster and let it dissolve back into the big sky. When the clouds and waves immediately return, it's no problem. We just acknowledge them again and again with unconditional friendliness, labelling them as just "thinking" and letting them go again and again and again.

Sometimes people use meditation to try to avoid bad feelings and disturbing thoughts. We might try to use the labelling as a way to get rid of what bothers us, and if we connect with something blissful or inspiring, we might think we've finally got it and try to stay where there's peace and harmony and nothing to fear. So right from the beginning it's helpful to always remind yourself that meditation is about opening and relaxing with whatever arises, without picking and choosing. It's definitely not meant to repress anything, and it's not intended to encourage grasping, either. Allen Ginsberg uses the expression "surprise mind." You sit down and—wham!—a rather nasty surprise arises. Okay. So be it. This part is not to be rejected but compassionately acknowledged as "thinking" and let go. Then—wow!—a very delicious surprise appears. Okay. So be it. This part is not to be clung to but compassionately acknowledged as "thinking" and let go. These surprises are, we find, endless. Milarepa, the twelfth-century Tibetan yogi, sang wonderful songs about the proper way to meditate. In one song he says that the mind has more projections than there are dust motes in a sunbeam and that even hundreds of spears couldn't put an end to that. So as meditators we might as well stop struggling against our thoughts and realise that honesty and humour are far more inspiring and helpful than any kind of solemn religious striving for or against anything.

E from atomic habits

Habits are the compound interest of self-improvement. The same way that money multiplies through compound interest, the effects of your habits multiply as you repeat them. They seem to make little difference on any given day and yet the impact they deliver over the months and years can be enormous. It is only when looking back two, five, or perhaps ten years later that the value of good habits and the cost of bad ones becomes strikingly apparent. This can be a difficult concept to appreciate in daily life. We often dismiss small changes because they don't seem to matter very much at the moment. If you save a little money now, you're still not a millionaire. If you go to the gym three days in a row, you're still out of shape. If you study Mandarin for an hour tonight, you still haven't learned the language. We make a few changes, but the results never seem to come quickly and so we slide back into our previous routines. Unfortunately, the slow pace of transformation also makes it easy to let a bad habit slide. If you eat an unhealthy meal today, the scale doesn't move much. If you work late tonight and ignore your family, they will forgive you. If you procrastinate and put your project off until tomorrow, there will usually be time to finish it later. A single decision is easy to dismiss.

But when we repeat 1 percent errors, day after day, by replicating poor decisions, duplicating tiny mistakes, and rationalising little excuses, our small choices compound into toxic results. It's the accumulation of many missteps—a 1 percent decline here and there—that eventually leads to a problem.

F from the psychology of money

Here's the thing: People from different generations, raised by different parents who earned different incomes and held different values, in different parts of the world, born into different economies, experiencing different job markets with different incentives and different degrees of luck, learn very different lessons. Everyone has their own unique experience with how the world works. And what you've experienced is more compelling than what you learn second-hand. So all of us—you, me, everyone—go through life anchored to a set of views about how money works that vary wildly from person to person.

What seems crazy to you might make sense to me. The person who grew up in poverty thinks about risk and reward in ways the child of a wealthy banker cannot fathom if he tried. The person who grew up when inflation was high experienced something the person who grew up with stable prices never had to. The stock broker who lost everything during the Great Depression experienced something the tech worker basking in the glory of the late 1990s can't imagine. The Australian who hasn't seen a recession in 30 years has experienced something no American ever has. On and on. The list of experiences is endless. You know stuff about money that I don't, and vice versa.

You go through life with different beliefs, goals, and

forecasts, then I do. That's not because one of us is smarter than the other, or has better information. It's because we've had different lives shaped by different and equally persuasive experiences.

G

"In a town of the steppes where I found life exceedingly dull, the best and the brightest spot was the cemetery. Often I used to walk there, and once it happened that I fell asleep on some thick, rich, sweet-smelling grass in a cradle-like hollow between two tombs.

From that sleep I was awakened with the sound of blows being struck against the ground near my head. The concussion of them jarred me not a little, as the earth quivered and tinkled like a bell. Raising myself to a sitting posture, I found sleep still so heavy upon me that at first my eyes remained blinded with unfathomable darkness, and could not discern what the matter was. The only thing that I could see amid the golden glare of the June sunlight was a wavering blur which at intervals seemed to adhere to a grey cross, and to make it give forth a succession of soft creaks.

Presently, however—against my wish, indeed—that wavering blur resolved itself into a little, elderly man. Sharp-featured, with a thick, silvery tuft of hair beneath his under lip, and a bushy white moustache curled in military fashion, on his upper, he was using the cross as a means of support as, with his disengaged hand outstretched, and sawing the air, he dug his foot repeatedly into the ground, and, as he did so, bestowed upon me sundry dry, covert glances from the depths of a pair of dark eyes.

H

If I were to look over the whole world to find out the country most richly endowed with all the wealth, power, and beauty that nature can bestow—in some parts a very paradise on earth—I should point to India. If I were asked under what sky the human mind has most full developed some of its choicest gifts, has most deeply pondered on the greatest problems of life, and has found solutions of some of them which well deserve the attention even of those who have studied Plato and Kant—I should point to India. And if I were to ask myself from what literature we, here in Europe, we who have been nurtured almost exclusively on the thoughts of Greeks and Romans, and of one Semitic race, the Jewish, may draw that corrective which is most wanted in order to make our inner life more perfect, more comprehensive, more universal, in fact more truly human, a life, not for this life only, but a transfigured and eternal life—again I should point to India.

Let me therefore explain at once to my friends who may have lived in India for years, as civil servants, or officers, or missionaries, or merchants, and who ought to know a great deal more of that country than one who has never set foot on the soil of Âryâvarta, that we are speaking of two very different Indias. I am thinking chiefly of India such as it was a thousand, two thousand, it may be three thousand years ago; they think of the India of to-day. And again, when thinking of the India of to-day, they remember chiefly the India of Calcutta, Bombay, or Madras, the India of the towns. I look to the India of the village communities, the true India of the Indians.

I

"We have a great deal more kindness than is ever spoken. Barring all the selfishness that chills like east winds the world, the whole human family is bathed with an element of love like a fine ether. How many persons we meet in houses, whom we scarcely speak to, whom yet we honour, and who honour us! How many we see in the street, or sit with in church, whom, though silently, we warmly rejoice to be with! Read the language of these wandering eyebeams. The heart knoweth.

2. The effect of the indulgence of this human affection is a certain cordial exhilaration. In poetry, and in common speech, the emotions of benevolence and complacency which are felt toward others, are likened to the material effects of fire; so swift, or much more swift, more active, more cheering are these fine inward irradiations. From the highest degree of passionate love, to the lowest degree of goodwill, they make the sweetness of life.

"3. Our intellectual and active powers increase with our affection. The scholar sits down to write, and all his years of meditation do not furnish him with one good thought or happy expression; but it is necessary to write a letter to a friend, and, forthwith, troops of gentle thoughts invest themselves, on every hand, with chosen words. See in any house where virtue and self-respect abide, the palpitation which the approach of a stranger causes. A commended stranger is expected and announced, and an uneasiness between pleasure and pain invades all the hearts of a household. His arrival almost brings fear to the good hearts that would welcome him. The house is dusted, all things fly into their places, the old coat is exchanged for the new, and they must get up for dinner if they can. Of a commended stranger, only the good report is told by others, only the good and new is heard by us. He stands to us for humanity"

J from the boom Sapiens

Biologists classify organisms into species. Animals are said to belong to the same species if they tend to mate with each other, giving birth to fertile offspring. Horses and donkeys have a recent common ancestor and share many physical traits. But they show little sexual interest in one another. They will mate if induced to do so – but their offspring, called mules, are sterile. Mutations in donkey DNA can therefore never cross over to horses, or vice versa. The two types of animals are consequently considered two distinct species, moving along separate evolutionary paths. By contrast, a bulldog and a spaniel may look very different, but they are members of the same species, sharing the same DNA pool. They will happily mate and their puppies will grow up to pair off with other dogs and produce more puppies. Species that evolved from a common ancestor are bunched together under the heading 'genus' (plural genera). Lions, tigers, leopards and jaguars are different species within the genus Panthera. Biologists label organisms with a two-part Latin name, genus followed by species. Lions, for example, are called Panthera leo, the species leo of the genus Panthera. Presumably, everyone reading this book is a Homo sapiens – the species sapiens (wise) of the genus Homo (man). Genera in their turn are grouped into families, such as the cats (lions, cheetahs, house cats), the dogs (wolves, foxes, jackals) and the elephants (elephants, mammoths, mastodons). All members of a family trace their lineage back to a founding matriarch or patriarch. All cats, for example, from the smallest house kitten to the most ferocious lion, share a common feline ancestor who lived about 25 million years ago.

Report Writing

How to write report in paper two:

A report is a formal writing detailed description about something that has been observed or a research. It is an organised presentation of the facts of an event that took place somewhere already.

Components of report writing

The structure of report has five parts

1 a heading

2 A byline telling about the writer, date and place of the event.

3. Lead which covers the most important facts.

4. Body which includes the detailed information.

5. Summary which concludes by a solution or a declaration by a prominent authority.

- on the left top corner, you need to mention three things one after another vertically. First is the name of the reporter second place from where it is reported in the last is the date of the report in the examination you can just write ABC or XYZ in the place of name of the reporter and the place can be your exam location or the location of the event and date can be your examination date or if given the specific date of the event.

- To avoid mistakes and to give clarity when should always divide the report in very short sentences like 3 to 4 lines.

- You can get the clarity of report writing from the reports of any good newspaper.

- There is a theory or rule of 5Ws that can be very helpful in a good report writing what, where, when, who, how. Which means what was the event? Where did it take place and when? Who was involved in the event? And how did the event happen?

- By just answering all these, you can get a good report out of it.

- Report is always written in the past tense.

- Be clear that the event has already happened and you are reporting the same event as a reporter.
- You must not be biased, and you just have to report the facts in a neutral manner.
- You can add relevant studies or reports of the relevant organisation, but it must be very relevant.
- Report must contain relevant statements from prominent authorities. Climate change policies.

Writing a 200-word report requires conciseness and clarity while still conveying the essential information. Here's a simple structure you can follow:

Format:

HEADLINE:

1. **Introduction (20-30 words)**:

- Start with a brief overview of the topic to provide context and grab the reader's attention.

2. **Main Body (150-160 words)**:

- Divide the body into two or three paragraphs, each focusing on a key aspect or point related to your topic.

- Provide facts, statistics, or examples to support your points.

- Keep sentences short and to the point, avoiding unnecessary details or repetition.

- Use transitional phrases to connect ideas smoothly.

3. **Conclusion (20-30 words)**:

- Summarize the main points discussed in the report.

- End with a thought-provoking statement or a call to action, depending on the nature of the topic.

Here's an example of how you could structure a 200-word report on the topic of "Climate Change Policies":

Climate Change Policies

ABC

The Times Of India

New Delhi

22-03-2025

Climate change poses a significant threat to the planet, prompting governments and organizations to implement policies aimed at reducing carbon emissions.

Recent initiatives such as the Paris Agreement have set targets for carbon reduction, with countries pledging to increase renewable energy adoption and decrease reliance on fossil fuels. Further many countries have enacted region specific laws to combat climate change. Laws have been placed to combat different types of pollution. However, challenges remain in meeting these goals, including political resistance and economic constraints. Despite these challenges, technological advancements in renewable energy and innovative policy approaches offer hope for progress in combating climate change. For example, carbon pricing mechanisms and investments in green infrastructure can incentivize sustainability while creating job opportunities.

It is important that governments and businesses collaborate to accelerate the transition to a low-carbon economy and mitigate the impacts of climate change. Civil society has an important role towards spreading awareness among the masses.

While climate change policies face obstacles, concerted efforts and innovative solutions can pave the way for a sustainable future. Prime Minister Sh Narendra Modi in his recent visit to the United States emphasised clearly on the issue of climate change and the two leaders pledged to work together on this issue.

Report topics

Here are several current affairs topics along with potential angles you could explore for a 200-word report:

1. **Climate Change Policies**: Analyze recent initiatives or international agreements aimed at combating climate change and their potential impacts on global carbon emissions and environmental sustainability.

2. **Global Health Crisis**: Investigate the latest developments in the fight against a specific disease outbreak (e.g., COVID-19 variants, vaccine distribution challenges) and their implications for public health strategies worldwide.

3. **Political Unrest**: Examine ongoing protests or conflicts in a specific region, discussing the root causes, key actors involved, and potential outcomes for political stability and human rights.

4. **Technological Advancements**: Explore recent breakthroughs in emerging technologies such as artificial intelligence, renewable energy, or space exploration, highlighting their potential to shape various industries and societies.

5. **Economic Trends**: Analyze the effects of recent economic policies or events (e.g., inflation rates, trade agreements, stock market fluctuations) on national and global economies, including implications for businesses and consumers.

6. **Social Justice Movements**: Investigate the progress and challenges faced by social justice movements advocating for equality and inclusion in areas such as race, gender, or LGBTQ+ rights, examining recent milestones and ongoing struggles.

7. **Geopolitical Tensions**: Assess the implications of recent diplomatic disputes or military conflicts between countries, considering potential consequences for regional stability, international relations, and humanitarian concerns.

8. **Environmental Conservation Efforts**: Discuss initiatives aimed at preserving biodiversity, combating deforestation, or protecting endangered species, highlighting recent successes and ongoing challenges in environmental conservation.

Choose a topic that interests you and dive into recent news articles, reports, and expert opinions to craft a concise yet informative report.

Some other topics for report:

1. Mid-day meal scheme
2. Hunger Crisis.
3. Global Hunger Index 2023.
4. Community Health Centres (CHCs)
5. Antimicrobial Resistance (AMR)
6. Palliative Care In India.
7. Euthanasia
8. India's Mental-Health Problem

9. Digital Health Adoption in India
10. Global Education Monitoring Report 2023
11. National Institutional Ranking Framework Rankings
12. National Credit Framework.
13. Mother Tongue in Foundational Education
14. Technology Interventions in Education.

Reading Comprehension

Reading comprehension is the ability to understand and make sense of written text, involving both decoding words and grasping the overall meaning, which is crucial for learning and success in various areas.

Key Aspects of Reading Comprehension:

- Decoding and Fluency:
- Reading comprehension relies on the ability to decode words accurately and fluently, allowing readers to focus on understanding the meaning.
- Vocabulary:
- A strong vocabulary is essential for understanding the meaning of words and sentences.
- Text Structure:
- Recognizing how sentences and paragraphs are organized helps readers understand the flow of ideas.
- Making Connections:
- Readers should be able to connect ideas within and between sentences and paragraphs, as well as relate the text to their own knowledge and experiences.
- Inferencing:
- Reading comprehension involves drawing inferences and making logical conclusions based on the text.
- Summarizing:
- Being able to summarize the main points of a text demonstrates comprehension.
- Critical Thinking:
- Reading comprehension involves evaluating the text, identifying the author's purpose, and forming your own opinions.

Q1. Read the following text and answer the questions that follow

The Centre is methodical. The recently tabled press and registration of periodicals bill, 2023 appeared to many to be a methodical step in destroying freedoms. The government, however, declared that the bill would simplify the process of registration presented in the Press and Registration of Books Act, 1867, which the new law will replace. It will aid transparency and ease of business and help small and medium publishers. But these uplifting goals have not prevented the government from opening up multiple centres of power that can decide the fate of journals.

The alarm expressed by the Editors Guild of India over the bill's 'draconian provisions' indicates how the bill threatens press freedom. The EGI has written about its areas of worry to the prime minister and highly-placed leaders and suggested that the bill be sent to a parliamentary select committee for discussion. 'Registration', not 'regulation', is what a free press requires.

The 1867 law empowered only the district magistrate to suspend or cancel the certificate of registration for a publication. The new law gives this power not only to the press registrar but also to other 'specific authorities', suggesting that law enforcement agencies, too, could butt in. The EGI fears the possibilities of arbitrariness and intrusiveness because any of these authorities can enter publishing premises to question people and seize documents. The bill seems to have built-in guarantees of compliance. Anyone accused of terrorist activity and of actions detrimental to the security of the State would be barred from publishing.

The ceaseless use of laws against terror and sedition is a constant threat to journalists, who are occasionally jailed. But criticism of the government was so far being suppressed by arresting individuals; the new law would ensure silence even before a line is published. Since the Centre will evolve guidelines for news publication, it could mean a full-blown shift from news to fairy-tale. Lightening the penal provisions of the 1867 Act is intriguing too.

An improper declaration of publishers and printers before the district magistrate will not matter. And the law will tread lightly when there is publication without registration, making it punishable if publishing continues for six months after warning. Who are the intended beneficiaries? A free press is one of the most precious freedoms the country enjoys. This is now at grave risk.

Answer the following Questions based on the above passage

I. What is the primary goal of the Press and Registration of Periodicals Bill, 2023, according to the government? 4 marks

Ans. The primary goal of the press and registration of periodical bill, 2023, according to the government is To simplify the process of press registration

II. Share evidence from the passage that supports the concern expressed by the Editors Guild of India (EGI) about the new bill. 4 marks

Ans: The passage mentions that the EGI has expressed alarm over the bill's 'draconian provisions' and suggested that it be sent to a parliamentary select committee for discussion.

III. Explain the potential implications of the new law on press freedom, as highlighted in the passage. 4 marks

Answer: The new law, by granting additional power to various authorities to suspend registrations and seize documents, may lead to arbitrary actions against the press. It could enable pre-publication censorship, hindering open criticism of the government.

IV. In the context of the passage, how does the new laws' focus on "registration" rather than "regulation" impact the concept of a free press? 4 marks

Answer: The emphasis on "registration" implies a bureaucratic process, potentially restricting the scope of a free press by creating barriers to entry and allowing authorities to exert control before publication.

V. State TRUE or FALSE. (4 M)

The new law is designed to lighten the penal provisions of the 1867 Act, making it easier for publishers to operate without strict oversight.

Answer: FALSE. The passage suggests that the new law may actually increase potential risks and barriers for publishers, including the possibility of arbitrary actions and pre-publication censorship.

Sample paragraphs for practice

This is a time to understand things. Fundamental things. Like do you and I understand the same things when we say the same things? Or are those things different things? Watan? Where is it? Show please. Where is it?

No please, not the map. And which map? There are many maps. Our maps. Their maps. Maps in atlases. Maps on negotiating tables. Maps on paper. Maps in our heads. Maps we are given. Maps we are kept from. Sanctioned maps. Maps that will violate sanction.

I am right in thinking — let me not say it out aloud, or on record, you know how things are these days with such things — that different people are right to imagine different shapes (or maps) of the watan? I mean there is the akhand watan, call it vision or imagination or ambition, but there is that notion of the akhand watan.

Then there is the vasudhaiv notion. The world in its entirety, not strictly a watan but a family, one family, the same family. Tough to tell how that happens. Especially given, you know... Just look around, you'll see if you do not already. The whole blooming world is a family? You must be either very funny or terribly cruel. Which probably reminds me of something worth mentioning. There is also the map that has been recently dented not in one place but several. Wonder what that makes the watan look like, nobody's telling because nobody really knows.

But watan is more than maps, a lot, lot more. Watan, more than anything else, is people. We are now the watan with the most people in it, which happened sometime ago. But this too is happening — a lot of people, thousands and thousands, are choosing to leave the watan for other watans. And many more are being asked to leave the watan by people belonging to this watan. Watan people telling other watan people to go away to another watan, very often one particular watan. We shall not name the watan because what is it of that watan, bhai? Then there is always this thing lurking in the works, this provision, like a promise to some and an apprehension to scores of others, that will by statute enable the extending of this watan people to other watans, it is not clear which. Meantime, what's approaching is this watan time (and also that watan time).

It is that sort of time. Watan time. We do these things at this time. Watan things.

You want to tell me

You are this nation bar all

I get it, oh I see

Oh I see in you our fall.

Answer the following questions:

I. Share evidence from the passage that suggests the complexity and ambiguity of the concept of "watan." (4 marks)

Answer: The passage discusses various maps of the watan, including those in atlases, on paper, and in people's heads. It also mentions the notion of the akhand watan and the vasudhaiv notion, highlighting the multifaceted nature of the concept.

II. Explain how the passage portrays the concept of "watan" as both inclusive and exclusive. (4 marks)

Answer: The passage explores the concept of "watan" through various maps and notions, reflecting the inclusiveness of a united family while acknowledging the exclusiveness and challenges of defining a nation.

III In the context of the passage, how does the concept of the "vasudhaiv notion" contrast with the idea of a single "akhand watan"? (4 marks)

Answer: The "vasudhaiv notion" represents a global unity and interconnectedness, while the "akhand watan" represents a unified and indivisible nation. The passage suggests that reconciling these notions can be challenging.

IV. State TRUE or FALSE. (4 marks)

The passage primarily focuses on the technical aspects of cartography and map-making.

Answer: FALSE. The passage delves into the philosophical and complex nature of the concept of "watan," encompassing notions of identity, unity, and belonging.

V. Select the option that best captures the central theme of the passage. (4 marks)

A. Exploring the concept of different maps and notions of "watan"

B. The history and evolution of maps in various contexts

C. The challenges of understanding and defining a nation

D. The importance of global unity and cooperation

Answer:: A. Exploring the concept of different maps and notions of "watan"

Are you taking good care of your liver? Signs that say you don't

The liver is a vital organ responsible for crucial bodily functions. It continuously produces bile, aiding fat-to-energy conversion which is important for digestion. It also removes toxins and harmful substances from the body, helping in regular purification. Overlooking its care can result in significant repercussions, often evident through subtle yet important signs. Here we list some symptoms that indicate whether your liver is in a bad shape, because recognizing these indicators is the initial step towards taking proactive measures to protect your liver and, by extension, your overall well-being.

A noticeable reduction in appetite can be an initial sign that your liver might not be functioning optimally. Sudden change in food or eating patterns and having an aversion to some of your favourite foods could also be a sign of your liver not being in good health. The liver's involvement in metabolism and digestion means its impairment can affect your desire to eat and enjoy meals.

Persistent feelings of vomiting, dizziness, and muscle pain can serve as a symptom of liver distress. As the liver aids in processing and removing waste products from the body, a malfunction will eventually lead to nausea symptoms because of the buildup of toxins in the bloodstream.

Terry's nails are a medical condition characterized by a specific appearance of the fingernails. In this condition, the nail beds (the area under the nails) appear pale or white, often with a narrow band of normal pink or reddish color at the tips. This can be caused by various underlying health issues, dominantly liver damage. The altered nail appearance is attributed to changes in blood supply and protein composition in the nails.

Porphyria Cutanea Tarda (PCT) is a condition where the skin gets easily hurt and forms painful blisters when exposed to sunlight. This happens because of certain proteins (porphyrins) building up in your liver and then moving into your blood and skin. These proteins make your skin very sensitive, especially when you're out in the sun. This excess porphyrin accumulates in the skin, making it sensitive and causing blisters, scars and increased hair growth.

Excessive insulin in the body due to insulin resistance, often associated with fatty liver disease and irregular liver function, can lead to acanthosis nigricans. This condition is characterized by darkening of the skin in certain areas like the neck crease, resulting from this surplus of insulin.

Experiencing discomfort or a dull ache in the upper right side of your abdomen could signify underlying liver inflammation or congestion. The discomfort might range from a mild, nagging sensation to a more pronounced and persistent ache, depending on the extent of liver involvement. Monitoring and assessing this discomfort can offer insights into potential liver health concerns that might need immediate medical attention.

Jaundice, recognizable by the yellowing of the eyes and skin, serves as a prominent indicator of compromised liver function. The liver's challenge in processing bilirubin, a yellow pigment derived from the breakdown of red blood cells, leads to its accumulation in the body, resulting in this distinctive discoloration. Bilirubin, typically metabolized and excreted by a healthy liver, can build up when the liver is not functioning optimally.

Ascites, the accumulation of excess fluid in the abdominal cavity, can result from diminished albumin production by the liver. Albumin, a crucial protein, helps regulate fluid balance. Ascites can cause discomfort, abdominal swelling, difficulty in day to day movements and difficulty breathing.

Normal stools derive their brown color from bile produced by the liver. If the liver isn't functioning optimally, it may produce inadequate bile, leading to pale or clay-colored stools. This alteration in stool color can serve as a noticeable indication of liver issues.

The liver plays a vital role in producing essential proteins necessary for blood clotting. However, when the liver is damaged, its ability to generate these clotting proteins is compromised. This reduction in clotting protein production leads to a heightened vulnerability to bruising even from minor injuries. Moreover, the impaired clotting mechanism results in prolonged bleeding from wounds that would typically clot swiftly.

If any of the above symptoms seem familiar, it is time to get checked by a medical professional to rule out any further complications and medicate as necessary

Answer the following questions on the basis of the passage above

I. Explain why the presence of acanthosis nigricans is associated with liver issues and what causes it.

II. How does jaundice affect the physical appearance of a person with liver issues?

III. Explain the role of the liver in processing waste products and its impact on feelings of vomiting and dizziness.

IV. Select the option that is similar in meaning to "Ascites."

    A) Accumulation of fluid in the lungs

    B) Accumulation of excess fluid in the abdominal cavity

    C) Accumulation of excess fat in the liver

    D) Accumulation of blood in the liver

V. Share evidence from the text to support the view that liver damage can lead to jaundice.

Grammar

Grammar forms the foundation of effective communication in the English language. In UPSC CAPF Paper 2, a strong grasp of grammar enhances reading comprehension, sentence correction, and logical reasoning through language-based questions. This section focuses on refining your understanding of essential grammar concepts—such as Nouns, Pronouns , tenses, Active Passive Voices, Direct-Indirect Speech, modifiers, prepositions, and sentence structure—so you can approach language-based questions with confidence and clarity. Practicing grammar regularly not only helps in scoring better in Paper 2 but also improves your overall articulation, both in written and verbal communication.

Nouns

Nouns: nouns are an essential part of speech that are used to refer to people, places, things, ideas, or concepts.

Common nouns: common nouns are used to refer to people, places, things and ideas in general sense. These are not written in capital. Examples are cat, tree, burger, hate, doctor etc.

Proper nouns: proper nouns are always written in capital irrespective of where they are in the sentence. These referred to specific people and places.

For example

Person: Ram

City: New York

Book: Pride and Prejudice

Company: Samsung

Holiday: Diwali

Concrete Nouns: refers to things that can be sense through our sense organs

Such as bed, grass, ice cream, scent, violin etc.

Abstract Noun: refers to things that cannot be perceived through a sense organs: for example grief, heartbreak, dictatorship, equality, fraternity, love

Countable nouns: things that can be counted in terms of singular or plural:

Examples include:

Pen- pens

Watch- watches

Orange- oranges

Uncountable nouns: things that cannot be counted and are always singular.

For example: air, water, salt, ocean, music

Collective nouns: refer to a group. Could be persons, things or animals

Example: a pair, a swarm, a herd, an army etc

Pronouns

Pronouns: pronouns are the parts of speech that can replace the nouns to make the speech more efficient and cohesive

Types:

1. Personal Pronouns: These refer to specific people or things (subject, object, or possessive):

- **Subject Pronouns:** I, you, he, she, it, we, they
  - Example: He went to the store.
- **Object Pronouns:** me, you, him, her, it, us, them
  - Example: The teacher gave me a book.
- **Possessive Pronouns:** mine, yours, his, hers, ours, theirs
  - Example: This book is mine.

2. Possessive Pronouns: These indicate ownership:

- my, mine, your, yours, his, hers, its, our, ours, their, theirs
  - Example: That car is his.

3. Reflexive Pronouns: These refer back to the subject of the sentence and end in "-self" or "-selves":

- myself, yourself, himself, herself, itself, ourselves, yourselves, themselves
  - Example: She hurt herself while playing.

4. Demonstrative Pronouns: These point out specific nouns or pronouns:

- this, that, these, those
  - Example: This book is interesting.

5. Interrogative Pronouns: These are used to ask questions:

- who, what, which, whom, whose

- Example: Who is coming to the party?

6. Relative Pronouns: These introduce noun clauses and connect them to the main clause:

- who, whom, whose, which, that, where, when
  - Example: The person who called is here.

7. Indefinite Pronouns: These refer to non-specific people or things:

- anyone, anyone, everything, nothing, someone, something, everyone, each, all, both, some, any, neither, either, one, nobody, no one, nothing, someone, something, everyone, each, all, both, some, any, neither, either, one, nobody, no one
  - Example: Someone knocked at the door

Fill the blanks with the correct form of pronouns.

1. We scored as many goals as ____ (they/them).
2. I am one year older than ____ (he/him).
3. He is as good a student as ____ (she/her).
4. Between you and ____ (I/me) he is a liar.
5. Let ____ (he/him) who can, save her from drowning.
6. The boy ____ (who/whom) fell off his bicycle and hurt his leg.
7. I have not seen the girl ____ (whose/whom) suitcase was stolen.
8. Seema is the maid ____ (who/whom) I have employed.
9. This is the paragraph about ____ (that/which) the teacher is talking about.
10. The letter ____ (which/what) he wrote reached me late.
11. The jury has given ____ (its/their) verdict.
12. The Cabinet gave ____ (their/its) vote.
13. The Secretary and Treasurer did not do ____ (their/his) job.
14. Each policeman and each homeguard was at ____ (their/his) post.
15. Neither John nor Tom has done ____ (their/his) work.
16. Either the leader or his followers did not do ____ (their/his) duty.

17. She and I completed _____ (our/ours) work.
18. Riya and _____ (myself/I) went to Kerela.
19. He _____ (that/whom) is down, need fear no fall.
20. She _____ (herself/themselves) saw the thief.

Answer:

1.	them
2.	he
3.	she
4.	me
5.	he
6.	who
7.	whose
8.	whom
9.	which
10.	which
11.	its
12.	their
13.	his
14.	his
15.	his
16.	their
17.	our
18.	I
19.	that
20.	herself

Verbs

Verbs: Verbs describe what a person or thing does or what is happening. Verbs are words that give the idea of action, of doing; something.

Types of Verbs:

1. **Helping verbs and main verbs:** Helping verbs or **auxiliary verbs** are verbs that have no meaning on their own. They are necessary for the grammatical structure of the sentence, but they do not tell us much alone.

    Example: People **must** start donating to charity.

    Main verbs are verbs that have a meaning of their own. They tell us something.

    Example: I **teach.**

2. **Transitive and intransitive verbs:** A transitive verb is one which must have an object to complete its meaning, and to receive the action expressed.

    For example: John **kicked** the ball.

    An intransitive verb is one which is complete in itself, or which is completed by other words without requiring an object.

    Example: John **talked.**

3. **Active and Passive Verbs:** The Active voice is the normal voice that we speak most of the time. In this voice the object receives the action of the verb performed by the subject.

    Example: Dogs eat bones.

    The Passive voice is less usual. In this voice the subject receives the action of the verb being performed by the object.

    Example: Bones are eaten by the dogs.

4. **Modal Verbs:** These verbs tell us whether something is probable or about the skills of a noun etc. There are 10 modal verbs in total and each has an important part in sentence formation.

Can, Could, May, Might, Will, Would, Must, Shall, Should, Ought to

5. **Dynamic and Static Verbs:** These verbs denote an actual action or expression or process done by the subject. They mean an action which can be seen or physically felt or the result of which is seen or physically felt by the object or an indirect object.

   Example: She **buys** new clothes every week.

   These verbs refer to the state of the subject or the situation of the subject. Stative Verbs tell us about the state of mind of the subject, or the relation between the subject and the object.

   Example: She **prefers** strawberry jam.

1. We _____ (has paid/have paid) him the money.
2. I _____ (have bought/has bought) my sister a watch.
3. _____ (Show/Shows) me your hands.
4. You _____ (has made/have made) your shirt dirty.
5. We _____ (are waiting/is waiting) for Rohan.
6. These books _____ (belong/belongs) to me.
7. She _____ (want/wants) to go.
8. We _____ (will like/would like) to visit the museum.
9. He _____ (has finished/have finished) talking.
10. My brother _____ (enjoy/enjoys) playing cricket.
11. We _____ (find/found) the house deserted.
12. We _____ (hope/hoped) that you would succeed.
13. She _____ (has assured/have assured) me that she is ready to help.
14. Nobody _____ (know/knows) when he will arrive.
15. We _____ (must find out/find) where to put it.
16. I _____ (shall show/show) you how to operate it.
17. Jack _____ (cannot/could not) decide what he should do next.

18. I _____ (can't/could not) imagine why she has behaved like that.

19. Can you _____ (tell/told/tells) me where he lives?

20. The club _____ (chose/chosen) Mr. Sam as the treasurer.

1.have Paid2.have bought3.Show4.have made5.are waiting6.belong7.wants8.would like9.has finished10.enjoys11.found12.hoped13.has assured14.knows15.must find out16.shall show17.could not18.can't imagine19.tell20.chose

Adverbs: **Meaning of adverb**

An **adverb** can modify a verb, an adjective, another adverb, a phrase, or a clause. An adverb indicates manner, time, place, cause, or degree and answers questions such as "how," "when," "where," "how much", etc.

While some adverbs can be identified by their characteristic *"ly"* suffix, most of them must be identified by untangling the grammatical relationships within the sentence or clause as a whole.

Adverb Examples:

The midwives waited *patiently* through a long labor.

He *literally* wrecked his car

Types of Adverbs: Definition and examples

1. **Adverb of time**

    An adverb of time tells us when something is done or happens.

    Example: Last week, we were stuck in the lift for an hour.

2. **Adverb of place**

    An adverb of place tells us where something is done or happens.

    Example: We can stop here for lunch.

3. **Adverb of manner**

    An adverb of manners tells us how something is done or happens.

    Example: The brothers were badly injured in the fight.

4. **Adverb of degree**

    An adverb of degree tells us the level or extent that something is done or happens.

Example: Her daughter is quite fat for her age.

5. **Adverb of frequency**

   An adverb of frequency tells us how often something is done or happens.

   Example: They were almost fifty when they got married.

Examples:

1. I'm going to tell you something very important, so please _____
2. Ann! I need your help. _____ !
3. They _____. At the end of the day they're always tired.
4. I'm tired this morning. I didn't _____ last night.
5. You're a much better tennis player than me. When we play, you always _____
6. _____ before you answer the question.
7. I've met Alice a few times but I don't _____ her very _____
8. Our teacher isn't very good. Sometimes he doesn't _____ things very _____

Answers:

1.	listen carefully.
2.	come quickly
3.	work hard
4.	sleep well
5.	win easily
6.	Think carefully
7.	know her very well
8.	explain things very clearly/well

Prepositions

A preposition is a word that connects nouns, pronouns, or noun phrases to other words in a sentence, showing relationships like time, place, or direction. Examples include "in," "at," "on," "of," "to," and "by".

Here's a more detailed explanation:

Function:

Prepositions establish relationships between words in a sentence, indicating things like:

- **Location:** "The book is on the table."
- **Time:** "She arrived after the movie started."
- **Direction:** "He drove over the bridge."
- **Object:** "She is looking for her keys."

Examples:

- **Single words:** in, at, on, of, to, by, with
- **Phrases:** in front of, next to, instead of

Common Prepositions:

- aboard, about, above, across, after, against, along, amid, among, around
- at, before, behind, below, beneath, beside, between, beyond, but, by
- despite, down, during, except, excluding, following, for, from, in, inside
- like, near, of, off, on, onto, outside, over, past
- than, though, to, toward, under, underneath, until, up, upon
- within, without

Preposition Practise Exercise

Complete the following exercises.

Fill in the blanks with appropriate prepositions

1. This shop doesn't have the toys I was looking __. (up/for)
2. The teacher divided the sweets ___ all the children. (between/among)
3. Bruce did not fare well __ his examination. (in/at)
4. The dog is grateful __ its owner. (to/for)
5. My brother's anniversary is __ 5th November. (on/in)
6. The boy __ the store is quite young. (at/on)
7. Mahatma Gandhi was born __ 2nd October. (on/in)
8. Rupert is fond __ muffins. (of/off)
9. The dog jumped __ the sofa. (on/in)
10. Humpty Dumpty sat __ a wall. (on/at)
11. The police officer is __ the station. (at/on)
12. The Sun will not rise __ 6 o'clock. (before/since)
13. I know Jack ___ he was a little boy. (for/since)
14. Priya's house is ___ mine. (next to/after)
15. The opponents sat ____ to each other. (opposite/behind)
16. The scientist looked ____ the microscope. (through/in)
17. I met Suhani when I was __ college. (in/on)
18. I will have completed my task __ Friday. (till/by)
19. There's a rift ___ these two kids. (between/among)
20. The soldiers are ___ war. (in/at)

Answers –

1. For
2. Among
3. In
4. To
5. On
6. At
7. On
8. Of
9. On
10. On
11. At
12. Before
13. Since
14. Next to
15. Opposite
16. Through
17. In
18. By
19. Between
20. At

Conjunction

A conjunction is a word that connects other words, phrases, or clauses within a sentence, acting as a bridge between ideas.

Here's a more detailed explanation:

Definition:

Conjunctions, also known as connecting words, join words, phrases, or clauses to create more complex and coherent sentences.

Types:

- **Coordinating Conjunctions:** These connect words, phrases, or clauses of equal grammatical rank, such as "and," "but," "or," "so," "for," "nor," and "yet". You can remember them using the mnemonic FANBOYS.

- **Subordinating Conjunctions:** These introduce dependent clauses (clauses that cannot stand alone) and connect them to independent clauses (clauses that can stand alone). Examples include "because," "although," "if," "when," "while," "as," "since," "until," and "though".

- **Correlative Conjunctions:** These are pairs of conjunctions that work together to connect words, phrases, or clauses, such as "either...or," "neither...nor," "not only...but also," and "both...and".

Examples:

- "I like pizza and cake." (Coordinating conjunction)
- "Because it was raining, we stayed inside." (Subordinating conjunction)
- "Either you can go, or I will." (Correlative conjunction)

Tenses

English grammar has 12 tenses, formed by combining three time periods (past, present, future) with four aspects (simple, continuous, perfect, and perfect continuous).

Here's a breakdown:

1. Simple Tenses:

Simple Present:

Describes habits, facts, and general truths.

- Example: "I eat breakfast every morning."

Simple Past:

Describes completed actions in the past.

- Example: "I ate breakfast this morning."

Simple Future:

Describes actions that will happen in the future.

- Example: "I will eat breakfast tomorrow."

2. Continuous Tenses:

Present Continuous:

Describes actions happening now or ongoing actions.

- Example: "I am eating breakfast right now."

Past Continuous:

Describes actions that were in progress at a specific time in the past.

- Example: "I was eating breakfast when the phone rang."

Future Continuous:

Describes actions that will be in progress at a specific time in the future.

- Example: "I will be eating breakfast at 8 am."

3. Perfect Tenses:

Present Perfect:

Describes actions that started in the past and continue to the present or have a result in the present.

- Example: "I have eaten breakfast."

Past Perfect:

Describes actions that were completed before another action in the past.

- Example: "I had eaten breakfast before the phone rang."

Future Perfect:

Describes actions that will be completed before a specific time in the future.

- Example: "I will have eaten breakfast by 8 am."

4. Perfect Continuous Tenses:

Present Perfect Continuous:

Describes actions that started in the past and are still ongoing or have a result in the present.

- Example: "I have been eating breakfast for an hour."

Past Perfect Continuous:

Describes actions that were in progress for a period of time before another action in the past.

- Example: "I had been eating breakfast for an hour before the phone rang."

Future Perfect Continuous:

Describes actions that will have been in progress for a period of time at a specific time in the future.

- Example: "I will have been eating breakfast for an hour by 8 am."

Choose the correct verb form from those in brackets:

1. Abdul _____ to be a doctor. (wants, wanting, is wanting)
2. The Soup _____ good. (taste, tastes, is tasting)
3. He _____ TV most evening. (watches, is watch, is watching)
4. He _____ out five minutes ago. (has gone, had gone, went)
5. When he lived in Hyderabad, he _____ to the cinema once a week. (goes, went, was going)

6. The baby _____ all morning. (cries, has been crying)

7. I _____ Rahim at the zoo. (saw, have seen, had seen)

8. I _____ Kumar this week. (haven't seen, did't see, am not seeing)

9. This paper _____ twice weekly. (is appearing, appearing, appears)

10. Ashok fell off the ladder when he _____ the roof. (is mending, was mending, mended)

11. I _____ something burning. (smell, am smelling, have been smelling)

12. Look, the sun _____ over the hills. (rises, is rise, is rising)

13. She _____ unconscious since four o'clock. (is, was, has been)

14. He used to visit us every week, but he _____ now. (rarely comes, is rarely coming, has rarely come)

15. I _____ him since we met a year ago. (didn't see, haven't seen, hadn't seen)

16. We _____ our breakfast half an hour ago. (finished, have finished, had finished)

17. She jumped off the bus while it _____ . (already started, had already started, would already start)

18. I _____ for half an hour when it suddenly started to rain. (have walked, have been walking, had been walking)

19. Did you think you _____ me somewhere before?. (have seen, had seen, were seeing)

20. The town _____ its appearance completely since 1980. (is changing, changed, has changed)

Answers

1.	Wants
2.	Tastes
3.	Watches
4.	Went
5.	Went
6.	Has been crying
7.	Saw
8.	Haven't seen
9.	Appears
10.	Was mending
11.	Smell
12.	Is rising
13.	Has been
14.	Rarely comes
15.	Haven't seen
16.	Finished
17.	Had already started
18.	Had been walking
19.	Had seen
20.	Has changed

Active Passive

Active Voice:

- Definition: The subject of the sentence performs the action.
- Structure: Subject + Verb + Object (SVO)
- Example: The dog (subject) chased (verb) the ball (object).

Rules for Active Voice:

1. Subject performs the action: In active voice, the subject is the doer of the action.
    - She writes the report. (She is performing the action of writing.)
2. Clarity and directness: Active voice tends to be clearer and more direct than passive voice.
    - He completed the assignment. (Clear and straightforward.)

Passive Voice:

- Definition: The subject of the sentence receives the action.
- Structure: Object + Verb (in past participle) + (by) Subject (SVO, with "by" optional)
- Example: The ball (object) was chased (verb) by the dog (subject).

Rules for Passive Voice:

1. Object becomes the subject: In passive voice, the object of the active sentence becomes the subject.
    - The letter was written by him. (The letter becomes the subject, while "him" is the agent of the action.)
2. Use of auxiliary verb: Passive voice often requires a form of "to be" (is, was, are, were, etc.) before the main verb in past participle form.
    - The book was read by her.
3. Agent (optional): The agent (the doer of the action) is sometimes omitted when it's unknown, irrelevant, or implied.
    - The cake was eaten. (No need to specify who ate it.)

4. Common in formal writing: Passive voice is often used in scientific or formal writing when the focus is more on the action or result than on who performed it.
   - The experiment was conducted in 1999.

Here are the rules for active and passive voice across all tenses:

---

1. Present Simple Tense
   - Active Voice:
   - Structure: Subject + Verb (base form) + Object
   - Example: She writes a letter.
   - Passive Voice:
   - Structure: Object + is/are + Verb (past participle)
   - Example: A letter is written by her.

---

2. Present Continuous Tense
   - Active Voice:
   - Structure: Subject + is/are + Verb (ing form) + Object
   - Example: She is writing a letter.
   - Passive Voice:
   - Structure: Object + is/are + being + Verb (past participle)
   - Example: A letter is being written by her.

---

3. Present Perfect Tense
   - Active Voice:
   - Structure: Subject + has/have + Verb (past participle) + Object
   - Example: She has written a letter.
   - Passive Voice:

- Structure: Object + has/have + been + Verb (past participle)
- Example: A letter has been written by her.

4. Present Perfect Continuous Tense
    - Active Voice:
    - Structure: Subject + has/have + been + Verb (ing form) + Object
    - Example: She has been writing a letter.
    - Passive Voice:
    - Structure: Object + has/have + been + being + Verb (past participle)
    - Example: A letter has been being written by her.

5. Past Simple Tense
    - Active Voice:
    - Structure: Subject + Verb (past form) + Object
    - Example: She wrote a letter.
    - Passive Voice:
    - Structure: Object + was/were + Verb (past participle)
    - Example: A letter was written by her.

6. Past Continuous Tense
    - Active Voice:
    - Structure: Subject + was/were + Verb (ing form) + Object
    - Example: She was writing a letter.
    - Passive Voice:
    - Structure: Object + was/were + being + Verb (past participle)
    - Example: A letter was being written by her.

7. Past Perfect Tense

- Active Voice:
- Structure: Subject + had + Verb (past participle) + Object
- Example: She had written a letter.
- Passive Voice:
- Structure: Object + had + been + Verb (past participle)
- Example: A letter had been written by her.

8. Past Perfect Continuous Tense

- Active Voice:
- Structure: Subject + had + been + Verb (ing form) + Object
- Example: She had been writing a letter.
- Passive Voice:
- Structure: Object + had + been + being + Verb (past participle)
- Example: A letter had been being written by her.

9. Future Simple Tense

- Active Voice:
- Structure: Subject + will + Verb (base form) + Object
- Example: She will write a letter.
- Passive Voice:
- Structure: Object + will + be + Verb (past participle)
- Example: A letter will be written by her.

10. Future Continuous Tense

- Active Voice:

- Structure: Subject + will + be + Verb (ing form) + Object
- Example: She will be writing a letter.
- Passive Voice:
- Structure: Object + will + be + being + Verb (past participle)
- Example: A letter will be written by her.

11. Future Perfect Tense
    - Active Voice:
    - Structure: Subject + will + have + Verb (past participle) + Object
    - Example: She will have written a letter.
    - Passive Voice:
    - Structure: Object + will + have + been + Verb (past participle)
    - Example: A letter will have been written by her.

12. Future Perfect Continuous Tense
    - Active Voice:
    - Structure: Subject + will + have + been + Verb (ing form) + Object
    - Example: She will have been writing a letter.
    - Passive Voice:
    - Structure: Object + will + have + been + being + Verb (past participle)
    - Example: A letter will have been being written by her.

General Guidelines for Passive Voice in All Tenses:
1. Object of the active sentence becomes the subject in the passive sentence.
2. Form of "to be": Use the appropriate form of the verb "to be" (am, is, are, was, were, will be, etc.) according to the tense.

3. Past participle of the main verb: The main verb in passive voice must always be in the past participle form.

4. Optional agent: The original subject (the doer of the action) is often omitted in passive voice if it's unknown, irrelevant, or implied.

Exercises from Passive Voice to Active Voice

Change the below sentences from Passive voice to Active voice:

1. The ball was kicked by the boy.
2. Dinner was cooked by the girl.
3. A lesson plan was written by the teacher.
4. The mailman was barked at by the dog.
5. The table was jumped on by the cat.
6. The meat was cooked by Sarath.
7. The essay was written by Salim.
8. The kennel was cleaned by the attendant.
9. The movie was directed by Christopher Nolan.
10. The chemistry book was read by the students.
11. The error was made by Andrew.
12. The rings were found by Catherine.
13. The proposal was denied by the board.
14. The book was written by Lewis Carroll.
15. The bold decision was taken by the CEO.

Answers:

1. The boy kicked the ball.
2. The girl cooked dinner.
3. The teacher wrote a lesson plan.
4. The dog barked at the mailman.

5. The cat jumped on the table.
6. Sarath cooked the meat.
7. Salim wrote the essay.
8. The attendant cleaned the kennel.
9. Christopher Nolan directed the movie.
10. The students read the chemistry book.
11. Andrew made the error.
12. Catherine found the rings.
13. The board denied the proposal.
14. Lewis Carroll wrote the book.
15. The CEO took the bold decision.

Exercises from Active Voice to Passive Voice

Change the below sentences from Active voice to Passive voice:

1. The carpenter built the house.
2. The reckless driver drove the car.
3. My grandmother baked the cake.
4. The committee wrote the report.
5. The manager sent the email.
6. The chef is preparing a delicious meal.
7. The engineers constructed a new bridge.
8. She will complete the assignment today.
9. People speak Portuguese in that colony.
10. The tide damaged the old dam.
11. The girls are solving maths problems.
12. A thief stole my car from the garage.
13. My mother planted beautiful flowers on the lawn.

14. The school awarded Bhavana the first prize.

15. Softtech Solution has developed a new software program.

Answers:

1. The house was built by the carpenter.

2. The car was driven by the reckless driver.

3. The cake was baked by my grandmother.

4. The report was written by the committee.

5. The email was sent by the manager.

6. A delicious meal is being prepared by the chef.

7. A new bridge was constructed by the engineers.

8. The assignment will be completed by her today.

9. Portuguese is spoken in that colony by people.

10. The old dam was damaged by the tide.

11. The maths problems are being solved by the girls.

12. My car was stolen from the garage by a thief.

13. Beautiful flowers were planted on the lawn by my mother.

14. Bhavana was awarded the first prize by the school.

15. A new software program has been developed by Softtech Solution.

Direct/Indirect

Direct Speech refers to the exact words spoken by a person, enclosed in quotation marks.

Example:

She said, "I am going to the market."

Indirect Speech (or reported speech) involves reporting what someone said without using their exact words. It does not use quotation marks and often changes the pronouns and verb tense.

Example:

She said that she was going to the market.

Key differences:

1. In direct speech, the words are quoted directly.
2. In indirect speech, the words are paraphrased and typically involve changes in verb tense, pronouns, and other elements.

Here are the rules for converting direct speech into indirect speech across different tenses:

1. Present Tenses in Direct Speech → Change to Corresponding Past Tenses in Indirect Speech

Direct Speech (Present)	**Indirect Speech (Past)**
Simple Present: He said, "I work hard."	Simple Past: He said that he worked hard.
Present Continuous: She said, "I am working."	Past Continuous: She said that she was working.

Present Perfect: They said, "We have finished."

Past Perfect: They said that they had finished.

Present Perfect Continuous: He said, "I have been working."

Past Perfect Continuous: He said that he had been working.

---

2. Past Tenses in Direct Speech → Change to Corresponding Past Forms in Indirect Speech

Direct Speech (Past)

Indirect Speech (Past)

Simple Past: She said, "I went home early."

Past Perfect: She said that she had gone home early.

Past Continuous: He said, "I was reading a book."

Past Perfect Continuous: He said that he had been reading a book.

Past Perfect: They said, "We had finished the project."

No Change: They said that they had finished the project.

Past Perfect Continuous: She said, "I had been studying all night."

No Change: She said that she had been studying all night.

---

3. Future Tenses in Direct Speech → Change 'Will' to 'Would'

Direct Speech (Future)

Indirect Speech (Past Future)

Simple Future: He said, "I will come tomorrow."

Future in the Past: He said that he would come the next day.

Future Continuous: She said, "I will be working at 5 PM."

Future Continuous in the Past: She said that she would be working at 5 PM.

Future Perfect: They said, "We will have finished by noon."

Future Perfect in the Past: They said that they would have finished by noon.

Future Perfect Continuous: He said, "I will have been studying for two hours."

Future Perfect Continuous in the Past: He said that he would have been studying for two hours.

---

4. No Change in Tense in Certain Cases

Tenses remain the same when:

- The reporting verb is in present/future tense:
- She says, "I like ice cream." → She says that she likes ice cream.
- He will say, "I am busy." → He will say that he is busy.
- The reported speech expresses a universal truth or habitual fact:
- The teacher said, "The sun rises in the east." → The teacher said that the sun rises in the east.
- He said, "Honesty is the best policy." → He said that honesty is the best policy.

---

5. Changes in Other Sentence Types

a) Questions

- Yes/No Questions → Use if/whether
- He asked, "Do you like coffee?" → He asked if/whether I liked coffee.
- WH- Questions → Retain the question word
- She asked, "Where do you live?" → She asked where I lived.

b) Imperatives (Commands/Requests/Suggestions)

- Commands → Use to + verb
- He said, "Close the door." → He told me to close the door.
- Negative Commands → Use not to + verb

- She said, "Don't touch it." → She told me not to touch it.
- Suggestions → Use suggested + that clause
- He said, "Let's go to the park." → He suggested that we go to the park.

In the following exercise, the given sentences are either in direct or indirect speech. Convert them into the opposite form of speech:

1. Sita said that she shall come to see the pictures.
2. I said to the teacher, "I am working hard."
3. The traveler said to me, "Can you tell me the way to the nearest inn?"
4. The teacher told me that I had not done my homework
5. Hari asked his father if he could go to the pictures that night
6. He said, "What a great misery!"
7. I said to the teacher, "I am sorry".
8. The merchant exclaimed with sorrow that he was ruined.
9. Ram will say that he saw his teacher in the park.
10. He said to me, "Trust in God and do the right."
11. He said that the man should come
12. He said to me, "You played very well yesterday."
13. He requested him to let him study.
14. She exclaimed that she loved chocolate ice cream.
15. I said that I had been ill since Monday.
16. He reminded us that the concert started at 7 PM.
17. I asked her if she wanted my help
18. The boy requested his papa to forgive him that time.
19. ."She is writing a novel," he mentioned.
20. He said, "She lives in Amritsar."

21. Mohan requested Rajan to go to the station with him.
22. Prem said to Pran, "Were you present at the meeting?"
23. The teacher said to the boy, "Shut the door."
24. The spectators said, "Bravo well played, Mohan!"
25. He said, "The train will be late."

Answers:

1. Sita said, "I shall come to see the picture."
2. I told the teacher I was working hard.
3. The traveler asked me if I could tell him the way to the nearest inn.
4. The teacher said to me, "You have not done your homework.
5. Hari said to the father, "May I go to the pictures tonight?"
6. He exclaimed that it was a great misery.
7. I told the teacher I was sorry
8. The merchant said, "Alas, I am ruined?"
9. Ram will say, "I saw my teacher in the park."
10. He advised me to trust in God and do the right.
11. He said, "The man shall come."
12. He told me that I had played very well the previous day.
13. He said to me, "Let me study."
14. "I love chocolate ice cream," she exclaimed.
15. I said, "I have been ill since Monday."
16. "The concert starts at 7 PM," he reminded us.
17. I said to her, "Do you want my help?"
18. The boy said, "Papa! Forgive me this time."
19. He mentioned that she was writing a novel.
20. He said that she lives in Amritsar.

21. Mohan said to Rajan, "Please go to the station with me."
22. Prem asked Pran if he had been present at the meeting.
23. The teacher asked the boy to shut the door.
24. The spectators applauded Mohan saying that he had played well.
25. He said that the train will be late.

Articles

Using Articles

What is an article? Basically, an article is an adjective. Like adjectives, articles modify nouns.

English has two articles: **the** and **a/an**. **The** is used to refer to specific or particular nouns; **a/an** is used to modify non-specific or non-particular nouns. We call the *definite* article and **a/an** the *indefinite article*.

the = definite article

a/an = indefinite article

For example, if I say, "Let's read **the** book," I mean a *specific* book. If I say, "Let's read **a** book," I mean *any* book rather than a specific book.

Here's another way to explain it: **The** is used to refer to a *specific* or *particular* member of a group. For example, "I just saw **the** most popular movie of the year." There are many movies, but only one particular movie is the most popular. Therefore, we use **the**.

"A/an" is used to refer to a *non-specific* or *non-particular* member of the group. For example, "I would like to go see **a** movie." Here, we're not talking about a *specific movie*. We're talking about *any* movie. There are many movies, and I want to see *any* movie. I don't have a specific one in mind.

Let's look at each kind of article a little more closely.

INDEFINITE ARTICLES: **A** AND **AN**

"A" and "an" signal that the noun modified is indefinite, referring to *any* member of a group. For example:

- "My daughter really wants **a** dog for Christmas." This refers to *any* dog. We don't know which dog because we haven't found the dog yet.
- "Somebody call **a** policeman!" This refers to *any* policeman. We don't need a specific policeman; we need any policeman who is available.

- "When I was at the zoo, I saw **an** elephant!" Here, we're talking about a single, non-specific thing, in this case an elephant. There are probably several elephants at the zoo, but there's only *one* we're talking about here.

REMEMBER, USING **A** OR **AN** DEPENDS ON THE SOUND THAT BEGINS THE NEXT WORD. SO...

- **a** + singular noun beginning with a consonant: *a boy; a car; a bike; a zoo; a dog*
- **an** + singular noun beginning with a vowel: *an elephant; an egg; an apple; an idiot; an orphan*
- **a** + singular noun beginning with a consonant sound: *a user* (sounds like 'yoo-zer,' i.e. begins with a consonant 'y' sound, so 'a' is used); *a university; a unicycle*
- **an** + nouns starting with silent "h": *an hour*
- **a** + nouns starting with a pronounced "h": *a horse*
    - In some cases where "h" is pronounced, such as "historical," you can use **an**. However, **a** is more commonly used and preferred.
    - A historical event is worth recording.

DEFINITE ARTICLE: **THE**

The definite article is used before singular and plural nouns when the noun is specific or particular. **The** signals that the noun is definite, that it refers to a particular member of a group. For example:

"**The** dog that bit me ran away." Here, we're talking about a *specific* dog, the dog that bit me.

"I was happy to see **the** policeman who saved my cat!" Here, we're talking about a *particular* policeman. Even if we don't know the policeman's name, it's still a particular policeman because it is the one who saved the cat.

"I saw **the** elephant at the zoo." Here, we're talking about a *specific* noun. There is only one elephant at the zoo.

COUNT AND NONCOUNT NOUNS

The can be used with noncount nouns, or the article can be omitted entirely.

- "I love to sail over **the** water" (some specific body of water) or "I love to sail over water" (any water).
- "He spilled **the** milk all over the floor" (some specific milk, perhaps the milk you bought earlier that day) or "He spilled milk all over the floor" (any milk).

"A/an" can be used only with count nouns.

- "I need **a** bottle of water."
- "I need **a** new glass of milk."

Most of the time, you can't say, "She wants a water," unless you're implying, say, a bottle of water.

GEOGRAPHICAL USE OF **THE**

There are some specific rules for using **the with** geographical nouns.

Do not use **the** before:

- names of most countries/territories: *Italy, Mexico, Bolivia*; however, *the*Netherlands, *the* Dominican Republic, *the* Philippines, *the* United States
- names of cities, towns, or states: *Seoul, Manitoba, Miami*
- names of streets: *Washington Blvd., Main St.*
- names of lakes and bays: *Lake Titicaca, Lake Erie* except with a group of lakes like *the Great Lakes*
- names of mountains: *Mount Everest, Mount Fuji* except with ranges of mountains like ***the** Andes* or ***the**Rockies* or unusual names like ***the**Matterhorn*
- names of continents (Asia, Europe)
- names of islands (Easter Island, Maui, Key West) except with island chains like **the** Aleutians, **the** Hebrides, or **the**Canary Islands

Do use **the** before:

- names of rivers, oceans and seas: ***the**Nile, **the** Pacific*
- points on the globe: ***the** Equator, **the**North Pole*
- geographical areas: ***the** Middle East, **the** West*

- deserts, forests, gulfs, and peninsulas: *the* Sahara, *the* Persian Gulf, *the* Black Forest, *the* Iberian Peninsula

OMISSION OF ARTICLES

Some common types of nouns that don't take an article are:

- Names of languages and nationalities: *Chinese, English, Spanish, Russian*(unless you are referring to the population of the nation: "**The** Spanish are known for their warm hospitality.")
- Names of sports: *volleyball, hockey, baseball*
- Names of academic subjects: *mathematics, biology, history, computer science*

Sample exercises

Complete the following sentences by filling in 'a' or 'an' or 'the' as may be suitable:-

1. Copper is ____ useful metal.
2. He is not ____ honourable man.
3. ____ reindeer is a native of Norway.
4. Honest men speak ____ truth.
5. Do you see ____ blue sky?
6. Aladdin had ____ wonderful lamp.
7. He returned after ____ hour.
8. ____ sun shines brightly.
9. ____ lion is ____ king of beasts.
10. You are ____ fool to say that.
11. French is ____ easy language.
12. Mumbai is ____ very dear place to live in
13. She is ____ untidy girl.
14. I bought ____ horse, ____ ox, and ____ buffalo.
15. If you see him, give him ____ message.
16. The guide knows ____ way.

17. Let us discuss ____ matter seriously.
18. Man, thou art ____ wonderful animal.
19. India is one of ____ most industrial countries in Asia.
20. He is ____ honour to this profession.

Answers

1.	a
2.	an
3.	the
4.	the
5.	the
6.	a
7.	an
8.	the
9.	the
10.	a
11.	a
12.	a
13.	an
14.	a, an, a
15.	the
16.	the
17.	the
18.	a
19.	the
20.	an

Gerunds and Infinitives

Gerunds and infinitives are verb forms that can take the place of a noun in a sentence. The following guidelines and lists will help you figure out whether a gerund or infinitive is needed.

Following a verb (*gerund or infinitive*)

Both gerunds and infinitives can replace a noun as the object of a verb. Whether you use a gerund or an infinitive depends on the main verb in the sentence. Consult the lists below to find out which form to use following which verbs.

I *expect* **to have** the report done by Friday. [INFINITIVE]

I *anticipate* **having** the report done by Friday. [GERUND]

Some common verbs followed by a gerund :

acknowledge	She *acknowledged* **receiving** assistance.
* accuse of	He *was accused of* **smuggling** contraband goods.
admit	They *admitted* **falsifying** the data.
advise	The author *advises* **undertaking** further study.
anticipate	He *anticipates* **having** trouble with his supervisor.

appreciate	I *appreciated* **having** a chance to read your draft.
avoid	He *avoided* **answering** my question.
complete	I finally *completed* **writing** my thesis.
consider	They will *consider* **granting** you money.
defer	She *deferred* **writing** her report.
delay	We *delayed* **reporting** the results until we were sure.
deny	They *denied* **copying** the information.
discuss	They *discussed* **running** the experiments again.
entail	This review procedure *entails* **repeating** the test.
* *look after*	He will *look after* **mailing** the tickets.
* *insist on*	He *insisted on* **proofreading** the article again.
involve	This procedure *involves* **testing** each sample twice.
justify	My results *justify* **taking** drastic action.
mention	The author *mentions* **seeing** this event.

plan on	They had *planned on* **attending** the conference.
postpone	The committee *has postponed* **writing the** report.
recall	I cannot *recall* **getting** those results before.
resent	He *resented* **spending** so much time on the project.
recommend	She *recommends* **reading** Marx.
resist	The writer *resists* **giving** any easy answers.
risk	She *risks* **losing** her viewing time.
sanction	They will not *sanction* **copying** without permission.
suggest	I *suggest* **repeating** the experiment.
take care of	He will *take care of* **sending** it to you.
tolerate	She can't *tolerate* **waiting** for results

Some common verbs followed by an infinitive:

afford	We cannot *afford* **to hesitate**.
agree	The professors *agreed* **to disagree**.
appear	The results *appear* **to support** your theory.
arrange	They had *arranged* **to meet** at noon.
beg	I *beg* **to differ** with you.
care	Would you *care* **to respond**?
claim	She *claims* **to have** new data.
consent	Will you *consent* **to run** for office?
decide	When did he *decide* **to withdraw**?
demand	I *demand* **to see** the results of the survey.
deserve	She *deserves* **to have** a fair hearing.
expect	The committee *expects* **to decide** by tomorrow.
fail	The trial *failed* **to confirm** his hypothesis.
hesitate	I *hesitate* **to try** the experiment again.
hope	What do you *hope* **to accomplish**?

learn	We have *learned* **to proceed** with caution.
manage	How did she *manage* **to find** the solution?
neglect	The author *neglected* **to provide** an index.
need	Do we *need* **to find** new subjects?
offer	We could *offer* **to change** the time of the meeting.
plan	They had *planned* **to attend** the conference.
prepare	He was not *prepared* **to give** a lecture.
pretend	I do not *pretend* **to know** the answer.
promise	They *promise* **to demonstrate** the new equipment.
refuse	She *refused* **to cooperate** any longer.
seem	Something *seems* **to be** wrong with your design.
struggle	We *struggled* **to understand** her point of view.
swear	He *swears* **to tell** the truth.

threaten	The team *threatened* **to stop** their research.
volunteer	Will you *volunteer* **to lead** the group?
wait	We could not *wait* **to hear** the outcome.
want	She did not *want* **to go** first.
wish	Do you *wish* **to participate**?

Following a preposition (*gerund only*)

Gerunds can follow a preposition; infinitives cannot.

Can you touch your toes *without* **bending** your knees?

He was fined *for* **driving** over the speed limit.

She got the money *by* **selling** the car.

A corkscrew is a tool *for* **taking** corks out of bottles.

Note: Take care not to confuse the preposition "to" with an infinitive form, or with an auxiliary form such as *have to*, *used to*, *going to*

He went back *to* **writing** his paper.	[PREPOSITION + GERUND]
I *used to* **live** in Mexico.	[AUXILIARY + VERB]
I *want* **to go** home.	[VERB + INFINITIVE]

Following an indirect object (*infinitive only*)

Some verbs are followed by a pronoun or noun referring to a person, and then an infinitive. Gerunds cannot be used in this position.

Some common verbs followed by an indirect object plus an infinitive:

ask	I must *ask* you **to reconsider** your statement.
beg	They *begged* her **to stay** for another term.
cause	His findings *caused* him **to investigate** further.
challenge	Wilkins *challenged* Watson **to continue** the research.
convince	Can we *convince* them **to fund** our study?
encourage	She *encouraged* him **to look** beyond the obvious.
expect	They did not *expect* us **to win** an award.
forbid	The author *forbade* me **to change** his wording.
force	They cannot *force* her **to reveal** her sources.
hire	Did the department *hire* him **to teach the** new course?
instruct	I will *instruct* her **to prepare** a handout.
invite	We *invite* you **to attend** the ceremony.

need	They *need* her **to show** the slides.
order	He *ordered* the group **to leave** the building.
persuade	Can we *persuade* you **to contribute again**?
remind	Please *remind* him **to check** the references.
require	They will *require* you **to submit** an outline.
teach	We should *teach* them **to follow standard** procedures.
tell	Did she *tell* him **to make** three copies?
urge	I *urge* you **to read** the instructions before you begin.
want	I do not *want* you **to have** an accident.
warn	Why didn't they *warn* me **to turn** down the heat?

Identify the Gerunds and/or infinitives in the following sentences:

1. They are likely to show up at any time.
2. The man denied committing the crime.
3. Their memories of traveling in Africa will stay with them forever.
4. He has always been afraid of flying.
5. Swimming is good for your health.

6. Would you mind passing me the sugar?
7. She promised to read the report as soon as possible.
8. I had a hard time explaining the situation to my husband.
9. She had some problems reading without glasses.
10. Paul gave up smoking five years ago.
11. What about going to the zoo tomorrow?
12. Barca is succeeding in winning the Spanish championship.
13. They had fun skiing.
14. My friend was happy to see me at the party.
15. He was ashamed to admit that he had lied.
16. It was very kind of you to help me.
17. She always wastes her time reading bad books.
18. We had no problem driving from the airport to the train station.
19. She hadn't expected this task to be so difficult.
20. It's no use taking a taxi. We'll be late anyway.
21. Don't forget to sign the document as soon as you are finished.
22. She made me feel like a real man.
23. Playing video games all the time is very boring.
24. She is fond of reading comics.
25. Alvaro admitted cheating during the English test.

Answers:
1. infinitive: to show
2. gerund: committing
3. gerund: traveling
4. gerund: flying
5. gerund: swimming

6. gerund: passing
7. infinitive: to read
8. gerund: explaining
9. gerund: reading
10. gerund: smoking
11. gerund: going
12. gerund: succeeding
13. gerund: skiing
14. infinitive: to see
15. infinitive: to admit
16. infinitive: to help
17. gerund: reading
18. gerund: driving
19. infinitive: to be
20. gerund: taking
21. infinitive: to sign
22. infinitive: to feel
23. gerund: playing
24. gerund: reading
25. gerund: cheating

Modal Verbs

Modal verbs, also known as auxiliary verbs, are special verbs that express concepts like possibility, ability, permission, obligation, or necessity, and are used alongside the main verb to modify its meaning. Common examples include "can," "could," "may," "might," "must," "shall," "should," "will," "would," and "ought".

Here's a more detailed explanation:

Function:

Modal verbs don't describe an action themselves, but rather they add nuance and context to the main verb, indicating the speaker's attitude or the likelihood of the action.

Examples:

- **Ability:** "I can swim" (possesses the ability)
- **Permission:** "You may leave" (is granted permission)
- **Obligation:** "You must pay the bill" (is required to pay)
- **Possibility:** "It might rain tomorrow" (is a possibility)

Auxiliary Verbs:

Modal verbs are also known as auxiliary verbs because they "help" the main verb by adding meaning and context.

Structure:

Modal verbs are followed by the base form of the main verb (e.g., "I can go," "You must study"

List of Modal Verbs

Must – to have to, or to be highly likely. Must can be used to express 100% certainty, a logical deduction or prohibition depending on the context.

- It *must* be hard to work 60-hours a week. (probable)
- You *must* listen to the professor during the lecture. (necessity)

- She *must not* be late for her appointment. (necessity)
- It *must not* be very hard to do. (probable)

Can – to be able to, to be allowed to, or possible. Can is a very common modal verb in English. It's used to express ability, permission and possibility.

- It can be done. (possible)
- She can sleepover at Sara's house this weekend. (allowed to)
- The car can drive cross country. (able to)
- It cannot be done. (impossible)
- The doctor said he cannot go to work on Monday. (not allowed to)
- She cannot focus with the car alarm going off outside. (not able to)

Could –to be able to, to be allowed to, or possible. Could is used when talking about an ability in the past or for a more polite way to ask permission.

- Mark could show up to work today. (possible)
- Could I come with you? (allowed to)
- When I was in college I could stay up all night without consequence. (able to)
- Mark could not come to work today. (possible/allowed)
- Last night I could not keep my eyes open. (able to)

May – to be allowed to, it is possible or probable

- May I sit down here? (allowed to)
- I may have to cancel my plans for Saturday night. (possible/probable)
- She may not arrive on time due to traffic. (possible)

Might – to be allowed to, possible or probable. Might is used when discussing something that has a slight possibility of happening, or to ask for permission in a more polite way.

- Chris might show up to the concert tonight. (possible/probable)
- Might I borrow your computer? (Many people don't say this in American English, instead they would say *Can I borrow your computer?* Or *May I borrow your computer?)*

Need – necessary

- Need I say more? (necessary)
- You need not visit him today. (not necessary)

Should – to ask what is the correct thing to do, to suggest an action or to be probable. *Should* usually implies advice, a logical deduction or a so-so obligation.

- Should I come with her to the dentist? (permission)
- Joe should know better. (advice/ability)
- It should be a very quick drive to the beach today. (possibility)
- Margaret should not jump to conclusions. (advice)

Had better – to suggest an action or to show necessity

- Evan had better clean up the mess he made. (necessity)
- Megan had better get to work on time tomorrow. (necessity)

Will – to suggest an action or to be able to

- John will go to his second period class tomorrow. (action)
- It will happen. (action)
- She will see the difference. (be able to)
- Eva will not drive the Volkswagen. (not do an action)
- Joe will not study tonight because he has to work. (not be able to)

Would – to suggest an action, advice or show possibility in some circumstances

- That would be nice. (advise/possibility/action)
- She would go to the show, but she has too much homework. (action)
- Mike would like to know what you think about his presentation. (action)

Exercise:

Fill in the blanks with the correct modal verb (can, could, may, might, must, should, shall, will, would)

1. I ___ finish my homework before dinner. (obligation)
2. Neha ___ take this white umbrella; it looks like it will rain. (advice)
3. ___ I borrow your pencil for a moment? (permission)
4. She ___ be home by now, but I'm not sure. (possibility)
5. If I were you, I ___ apologize immediately. (suggestion)
6. They ___ be here any minute. (certainty)
7. He said he ___ help me with my project next week. (future intention)
8. ___ you like some coffee? (offer)
9. We ___ leave early tomorrow for the trip. (necessity)
10. You ___ not speak to strangers. (prohibition)

Answers:

1. must (I must finish my homework before dinner.)
2. should (Neha should take this umbrella; it looks like it will rain.)
3. May (May I borrow your pencil for a moment?)
4. might (She might be home by now, but I'm not sure.)
5. would (If I were you, I would apologize immediately.)
6. must (They must be here any minute.)
7. will (He said he will help me with my project next week.)
8. Would (Would you like some coffee?)
9. must (We must leave early tomorrow for the trip.)
10. must (You must not speak to strangers.)

Sample Papers

1.

Q1Essay : write any 4 (80 marks)

A. The Indian Judiciary Needs Comprehensive Reforms to Ensure Timely Justice.

B. India's Policy of Non-Alignment is No Longer Relevant in the Current Global Scenario

C. The Indian Education System Stifles Creativity and Innovation

D. Tourism in India is Underdeveloped Despite its Potential.

E. The Future of Artificial Intelligence in India

F. Challenges and Solutions for Public Health in Rural India

Q2 Arguments (40 marks)

1. Euthanasia should be legalised in India
2. Governments should implement a tax on wealth rather than just income

Q3 Reports: (20 marks)

1. Bhartiya Nyaya Sanhita
2. Bioethanol production in India

Q4 Precis: one third of its length (15 marks)

The entire country was upended. Vast stretches of field, paddy, forest, and village were commandeered without warning for laying tracks. The Japanese and Korean governments had signed a treaty, but having already lost their national sovereignty, the Korean government officials were mere agents, tools of the Japanese colonisers. The Japanese railroad company didn't stop at seizing the land alongside the tracks, but also designated large areas of land around the stations as belonging to the railroad. They claimed at first that they would reward the landowners at one-tenth the cost of their land, but following their declaration of war against Russia, the army simply took the land without any further pretence. With the Japanese army at their back, the Gyeongbu Railway Company engineers, the Japanese civil-engineering companies contracted by them, and the rail workers themselves took the land needed for the railway by force. The land grabbing worsened along the Gyeongui Line. Everywhere the rails went, thousands upon thousands of common folk found themselves kicked off their land. It was theft, no question about it. Even the piddling compensation that was offered as hush money in the early days went instead to lining the pockets of provincial bureaucrats and petty government officials. The common folk lost not only their land but also their homes, forests, and even their ancestors' graves, for almost nothing in return. Laying the Gyeongbu rail lines was a way for Japan, which had only recently modernised, to make up for its weak capital base by plundering all that land for the rails.

Q5 Comprehension: (20 marks)

Read the passage given below:

1. Thackeray reached Kittur along with a small British army force and a few of his officers. He thought that the very presence of the British on the outskirts of Kittur would terrorise the rulers and people of Kittur, and that they would lay down their arms. He was quite confident that he would be able to crush the revolt in no time. He ordered that tents be erected on the eastern side for the fighting forces, and a little away on the western slopes tents be put up for the family members of the officers who had accompanied them. During the afternoon and evening of 20th October, the British soldiers were busy making arrangements for these camps.

2. On the 21st morning, Thackeray sent his political assistants to Kittur fort to obtain a written assurance from all the important officers of Kittur rendering them answerable for the security of the treasury of Kittur. They, accordingly, met Sardar Gurusiddappa and other officers of Kittur and asked them to comply with the orders of Thackeray. They did not know that the people were in a defiant mood. The commanders of Kittur dismissed the agent's orders as no documents could be signed without sanction from Rani Chennamma.

3. Thackeray was enraged and sent for the commander of the Horse Artillery, which was about 100 strong, and ordered him to rush his artillery into the fort and capture the commanders of Desai's army. When the Horse Artillery stormed into the fort, Sardar Gurusiddappa, who had kept his men on full alert, promptly commanded his men to

repel and chase them away. The Kittur forces made a bold front and overpowered the British soldiers.

4. In the meanwhile, the Desai's guards had shut the gates of the fort and the British Horse Artillerymen, being completely overrun and routed, had to get out through the escape window. Rani's soldiers chased them out of the fort, killing a few of them until they retreated to their camps on the outskirts.

5. A few of the British had found refuge in some private residences, while some were hiding in their tents. The Kittur soldiers captured about forty persons and brought them to the palace. These included twelve children and a few women from the British officers' camp. When they were brought in the presence of the Rani, she ordered the soldiers to be imprisoned. For the women and children she had only gentleness and admonished her soldiers for taking them into custody. At her orders, these women and children were taken inside the palace and given food and shelter. Rani came down from her throne, patted the children lovingly and told them that no harm would come to them.

6. She, then, sent word through a messenger to Thackeray that the British women and children were safe and could be taken back any time. Seeing this noble gesture of Rani, he was moved. He wanted to meet this gracious lady and talk to her. He even thought of trying to persuade her to enter into an agreement with the British to stop all hostilities in lieu of an inam (prize) of eleven villages. His offer was dismissed with a gesture of contempt. She had no wish to meet Thackeray. That night she called Sardar Gurusiddappa and other leading Sardars, and after discussing all the issues came to the conclusion that there was no point in meeting Thackeray who had come with an army to threaten Kittur into submission to British sovereignty.

QA On the basis of your understanding of the above passage, complete the statements given below with the help of options that follow: (4 marks)

(a) Thackeray was a/an

(i) British tourist

(ii) army officer

(iii) advisor to the Rani of Kittur

(iv) treasury officer

(b) British women and children came to Kittur to

(ii) enjoy life in tents

(iii) stay in the palace

(iv) give company to officers

QB Why did the Kittur officials refuse to give the desired assurance to Thackeray?

QC What happened to the Horse Artillery?

QD How do we know that Rani was a noble queen?

QE How, in your opinion, would the British women have felt after meeting Rani?

Q6 Do as directed (10 marks)

1. My neighbourhood is _____ very interesting place. My house is located _____ an area which has many stores and offices. [Fill in the blanks with articles and prepositions]

2. I don't know when he departed. [Turn into a simple sentence]

3. Yesterday, he came to my house when I _____ (study). [Fill in the blanks with the correct form of verbs]

4. Over exercise causes harm to our health. [Replace the underlined word with the correct phrasal verb]

5. The centre constituted a high-level technical team to resolve ___ Cauvery water dispute _____ Karnataka and Tamil Nadu. [Fill in the blanks with articles and prepositions]

6. We should not show cruelty to animals. [Rewrite using the adjective form of the underlined words]

7. The mother said to her son, 'Where have you been throughout the day?' [Turn into indirect speech]

8. The girl has kept the promise. [Change the voice]

9. Rina is the most intelligent girl in the class. [Rewrite using a positive degree of the adjective]

10. Always save some money for the future. [Replace the underlined word with the correct phrasal verb]

Q7 Fill in the blanks (5 marks)

1. When teaching my daughter how to drive, I told her if she didn't hit the ____ in time she would ____ the car's side mirror.(brake/break)

2. If you ____ drugs, you will get arrested and end up in a prison ____.(cell/sell)

3. If the ____ breaks on your shoe, you might fall. However, your injuries will ____ over time. (heal/heel)

4. I need to get a new ____ put on my favourite pair of running shoes. Jogging is good for my ____. (sole/soul)

5. I don't know ____ to bring a jacket or not. The ____ looks unpredictable today.(weather/whether)

Q8 Fill in the blanks with the appropriate form of modals.(5 marks)

1) He knew that he _____ (Would/ must) be able to reach office in time.

2) You _____ (dare/ could) not enter my house again.

3) I thought he _____ (should/ would) be at school.

4) Raman _____ (can/ should) speak in two voices.

5) I _____ (can't/ couldn't) write what you spoke.

Q9 . choose the correct idiom/phrase

I. He has the gift of the gab.

a. He is gifted

b. He is a chatterbox

c. He is a good conversationalist

II. Parental property has become a bone of contention between the siblings.

a. unifying factor

b. cause of quarrel

c. cause of rivalry

III. Once in a blue moon, we meet each other.

a. Frequently

b. Sometimes

c. Very seldom indeed

IV. He has been jobless for several months, and it is his wife who keeps the pot boiling.

a. Avoids starvation

b. Keeps firing

c. Gets angry

V. In the end he had to eat the humble pie.

a. apologize humbly

b. defend himself vigorously

c. adopt an aggressive attitude

2.

Q1 Essay : write any 4 (80 marks)

A. The implementation of the Citizenship Amendment Act (CAA) will have positive effects on India's refugee policy.

B. Insurgency in Jammu and Kashmir: historical context and current challenges

C. Environmental ethics in Indian philosophy

D. The role of India and China in global governance

E. Role of artificial intelligence in governance

F. Censorship is necessary to protect the society from harmful ideas

Q2 Arguments (40 marks)

1. The death penalty should be abolished in India
2. India's healthcare system needs more privatisation to improve efficiency and accessibility

Q3 Reports: (20 marks)

1. Bharat's MSME Boom
2. International Space Station

Q4 Precis: one third of its length (15 marks)

Reading is a fundamental skill that plays a vital role in our lives. It's not just about deciphering words on a page but about the doors it opens, the knowledge it imparts, and the worlds it allows us to explore. Reading is an essential tool for learning, expanding our horizons, and fostering imagination.

When we read, we acquire knowledge. Whether it's reading textbooks, newspapers, or online articles, we gain information that helps us understand the world. Books, in particular, are a treasure trove of knowledge. They contain the wisdom of generations, the discoveries of great minds, and the stories of diverse cultures. Reading books can educate us on history, science, literature, and countless other subjects. It's like having a mentor, guiding us through the complexities of life.

Reading also broadens our horizons. It exposes us to different viewpoints, perspectives, and experiences. When we read about characters from various backgrounds or explore far-off lands through the pages of a novel, we step into their shoes and see the world from a different angle. This broadening of perspective fosters empathy and understanding, making us more tolerant and open-minded individuals.

Q5 Comprehension: (20 marks)

Read the passage given below:

Can you imagine a college without walls, professors or classrooms? Educator Bunker Roy can. More than 40 years ago, Roy, now 69, founded the Barefoot College in Tilonia, Rajasthan. His school admits rural women, often grandmothers and teaches them the basics of solar engineering and freshwater technology. His efforts have yielded enormous benefits. When the women return to their homes, they are trained enough to provide their communities, some of the world's most lonely places, with electricity and clean water. They also gain something important: a newfound self-confidence. The Barefoot model has already been used to empower women throughout Asia, Africa, and Latin America. Last year, former President Bill Clinton presented Roy with a Clinton Global Citizen Award, which honours leaders who are solving the world's problems in effective ways.

2. If you go all over the world, to very remote villages, you will often find only very old people and very young people. The men have already left. So two ideas were put into practice in order to make the Barefoot Model work. First it was declared that men are untrainable, restless, always ready to move, ambitious, and they all want a certificate to show for their efforts. And the moment you give one of them a certificate, he leaves the village looking for a job in the city. That is how, the simple, practical solution of training grandmothers came up. They are sympathetic, tolerant, willing to learn, and patient. All the qualities you need are there. And the second idea was not to give out certificates. Because the moment a certificate is given, a woman, like a man, will see it as a passport for leaving rural areas and going to urban areas to find a job.

3. Barefoot College follows the lifestyle of Mahatma Gandhi: Students eat, sleep, and work on the floor. They can work for 20 years or they can go home the next day. As of today, 604 women solar engineers from 1083 villages in 63 countries have been trained. The engineers have given solar power to 45,000 houses. These were done by women who had never left their homes before. They hate the idea of leaving their

families and getting on a plane. When they reach India, sometimes after 19 hours of travel, they are faced with strange food, strange people, and a strange language. All the training is done in sign language. Yet in six months, they will know more about solar engineering than most university graduates. Some women face problems at home while attending college. Most of the husbands do not like their wives going to these colleges and tell them not to come back if they do so. But, on her return when she is able to help provide her village with solar electricity, her husband wants her to get back home. The respect she now has is enormous and she considers herself no less than solar engineers. Bunker Roy dreams of providing the world's 47 least developed countries with Barefoot College trained grandmothers and solar electrify more than 1,00,000 houses.

Answer the following questions briefly: 5X4=20

a. How is Barefoot College different from other colleges?

b. What did the women gain from the college apart from technology?

c. What are the difficulties the women have to face during their travel and their life in Tilonia, Rajasthan?

d. How do the women consider themselves professionally, after their training?

e. What is the narrator's dream about solar electrification?

Q6 Do as directed (10 marks)

1. It is probable that he will never come back. (Begin: In …)

2. He said to me, 'Where are you going?' (Begin: He asked me …)

3. As soon as the chief guest had arrived the play began. (Begin: No sooner ….)

4. I was surprised at his behaviour. (Begin: His …)

5. He will certainly succeed. (Begin: He is …)

6. He is the best student in the class. (Use better instead of best)

7. He is too weak to stand up without help.

8. He tucked the gun under his arm and rushed towards the bridge. (End: … his arm.)

9. We were late. Consequently, we missed the train. (Rewrite with as or since)

10. Though I had a headache, I enjoyed the movie. (Rewrite with in spite of)

Q7 Make sentences for the following idioms to illustrate their meaning (5)

a. To build a castle in the air

b. To beat around the bush

c. Birds of a feather

d. All's well that ends well

e. Every dark cloud has a silver lining

Q8 Fill in the blanks with the appropriate form of modals.(5 marks)

a. _____ you please keep the noise down? I'm trying to concentrate. (Can / Would / Should)

b. You _____ not park here; it's a no-parking zone. (may / should / must)

c. They _____ finish the project on time; they're working hard. (should / might / will)

d. _____ you please pass the salt? (will / can / could)

e. I _____ help you if I could. (will / would / might)

Q9 Insert a preposition, where necessary

a. He asked his father ………………………….. money.

b. They paid me …………………………. the books.

c. I thought he would offer Ann the job, but he offered it ………………………….. me.

d. Keep me a place, and keep a place ………………………….. Ann too.

e. They showed us photographs …………………………. their baby.

3.

Q1 Essay : write any 4 (80 marks)

a. Fiscal Policy and Its Role in India's Economic Stability

b. Desertification and Land Degradation in India: Causes and Mitigation

c. Role of the Media in Indian Democracy

d. Bhakti Movement: Philosophical Underpinnings and Social Impact

e. Drug Trafficking and Its Impact on India's Internal Security

f. Geopolitical Implications of India-China Relations

Q2 Arguments (40 marks)

1. Euthanasia should be legalised in India
2. Governments should implement a tax on wealth rather than just income

Q3 Reports: (20 marks)

1. India's Forex Reserve
2. Technology Interventions in Education.

Q4 Precis: one third of its length (15 marks)

Sometimes we feel guilty, sometimes arrogant. Sometimes our thoughts and memories terrify us and make us feel totally miserable. Thoughts go through our minds all the time, and when we sit, we are providing a lot of space for all of them to arise. Like clouds in a big sky or waves in a vast sea, all our thoughts are given the space to appear. If one hangs on and sweeps us away, whether we call it pleasant or unpleasant, the instruction is to label it all "thinking" with as much openness and kindness as we can muster and let it dissolve back into the big sky. When the clouds and waves immediately return, it's no problem. We just acknowledge them again and again with unconditional friendliness, labelling them as just "thinking" and letting them go again and again and again.

Sometimes people use meditation to try to avoid bad feelings and disturbing thoughts. We might try to use the labelling as a way to get rid of what bothers us, and if we connect with something blissful or inspiring, we might think we've finally got it and try to stay where there's peace and harmony and nothing to fear. So right from the beginning it's helpful to always remind yourself that meditation is about opening and relaxing with whatever arises, without picking and choosing. It's definitely not meant to repress anything, and it's not intended to encourage grasping, either. Allen Ginsberg uses the expression "surprise mind." You sit down and—wham!—a rather nasty surprise arises. Okay. So be it. This part is not to be rejected but compassionately acknowledged as "thinking" and let go. Then—wow!—a very delicious surprise appears. Okay. So be it. This part is not to be clung to but compassionately acknowledged as "thinking" and let go. These surprises are, we find, endless. Milarepa, the twelfth-century Tibetan yogi, sang wonderful songs about the proper way to meditate. In one song he says that the mind has more projections than there are dust motes in a sunbeam and that even hundreds of spears couldn't put an end to that. So as meditators we might as well stop struggling against our thoughts and realise that honesty and humour are far more inspiring and helpful than any kind of solemn religious striving for or against anything.

Q5 Comprehension: (20 marks)

Read the passage given below:

1. Today's woman is a highly self-directed person, alive to the sense of her dignity and the importance of her functions in the private domestic domain and the public domain of the world of work. Women are rational in approach, careful in handling situations and want to do things as best as possible. The Fourth World Conference of Women held in Beijing in September 1995 had emphasized that no enduring solution of society's most threatening social, economic and political problems could be found without the participation and empowerment of the women. The 1995 World Summit for Social Development had also emphasised the pivotal role of women in eradicating poverty and mending the social fabric.

2. The Constitution of India had conferred on women equal rights and opportunities political, social, educational and of employment with men. Because of oppressive traditions, superstitions, exploitation and corruption, a majority of women are not allowed to enjoy the rights and opportunities, bestowed on them. One of the major reasons for this state of affairs is the lack of literacy and awareness among women. Education is the main instrument through which we can narrow down the prevailing

inequality and accelerate the process of economic and political change in the status of women.

3. The role of women in a society is very important. Women's education is the key to a better life in the future. A recent World Bank study says that educating girls is not a charity, it is good economics and if developing nations are to eradicate poverty, they must educate the girls. The report says that the economic and social returns on investment in education of the girls considerably affect the human development index of the nation. Society would progress only if the status of women is respected and the presence of an educated woman in the family would ensure education of the family itself. Education and empowerment of women are closely related.

4. Women's education has not received due care and attention from the planners and policymakers. The National Commission for Women has rightly pointed out that even after 50 years of independence, women continue to be treated as the single largest group of backward citizens of India. The role of women in overall development has not been fully understood nor has it been given its full weight in the struggle to eliminate poverty, hunger, injustice and inequality at the national level. Even when we are at the threshold of the 21st century, our society still discriminates against women in matters of their rights and privileges and prevents them from participating in the process of national and societal progress.

Various Committees and Commissions have been constituted before and after the independence to evaluate the progress in women's education and to suggest ways and means to enhance the status of women. The female literacy rate has gone up in the 20th century from 0.6 per cent in 1901 to 39.29 per cent in 1991 but India still possesses the largest number of illiterate women in the world. The female literacy index for the year 1991 shows that there are eight States which fall below the national average. The most populous States of the country, UP, MP, Bihar and Rajasthan fall in the category of most backward States as far as female literacy is concerned.

5. The prevailing cultural norms of gender behaviour and the perceived domestic and reproductive roles of women tend to affect the education of girls. Negative attitude towards sending girls to schools, restrictions on their mobility, early marriage, poverty and illiteracy of parents affect the girl's participation in education.

6. Women's political empowerment got a big boost with the Panchayati Raj Act of 1993 which gave them 30 per cent reservation in Village Panchayats, Block Samities

and Zila Parishads throughout the country. The National Commission for Women was also set up in 1992 to act as a lobby for women's issues.

7. The educational system is the only institution which can counteract the deep foundations of inequality of sexes that are built in the minds of people through the socialization process. Education is the most important instrument of human resource development. Educational system should be used to revolutionize the traditional attitudes and inculcate new values of equality.

(i) Mention any two attributes of a modern woman.

(ii) Why are women's participation and empowerment considered necessary?

(iii) Which factors adversely affect the education of girls?

(iv) What benefits did the women get with the enactment of the Panchayati Raj Act of 1993?

(v) By what process can we remove the sense of inequality of sexes from the minds of the people?

Q6 Write one word for the following group of words.(5 marks)

1. That which cannot be heard.
2. One who believes in fate
3. A cure of all diseases.
4. One who speaks for others.
5. A period of a hundred years.

Q7 Do as directed (10 marks)

1. We shall not achieve our goals if we do not take action to achieve them. (Use 'unless')
2. We must have a clear picture in mind and must have the ability to adhere to that picture. (Use 'not only…..but also')
3. He felt the heat because he had not eaten since the previous nightfall. (Use 'so')
4. Mrs. Bhushan said, "I've been looking for you for almost an hour." (Change into indirect speech)

5. He's with the bank just now but they aren't giving him his pay. (Use 'Though')

6. Shwetha is a very beautiful girl. (Make it exclamatory)

7. It was cold but we went swimming. (Rewrite with although)

8. The tea was so hot that I could not drink it. (Use 'too')

9. He is too arrogant to listen to advice. (Use so...that)

10. He worked hard so that he might pass the examination. (Use 'to')

Q8 Fill in the blanks (5 marks)

1. Keep walking (strait/straight) until you reach Lincoln Blvd.

2. All the leaders claimed that they wanted (peace/piece).

3. Don't iron your clothes on the table; use an ironing (board/bored)!

4. Lord Williams hardly ever left his (manor/manner).

5. That lion has a beautiful (main/mane).

Q9 Fill in the blanks with the appropriate form of modals.(5 marks)

1. You _____ not touch that vase, it's very fragile. (must / may not / can)

2. We _____ leave early tomorrow if we want to avoid the traffic. (may / can / should)

3. There's a chance it _____ rain later this afternoon. (might / ought to / will)

4. _____ you please open the window? (could / should/ might)

5. You _____ get more exercise. It's good for your health. (should / must / need)

4.

Q1 Essay : write any 4 (80 marks)

A. Impact of Fake News and Misinformation on Internal Security

B. Developed country ambitions need deep structural reforms

C. An ageing India: The magnitude and the multitude

D. When AI weds molecular biology, miracle treatments are born

E. India's Leap Towards Green Energy

F. Caste system in India: Historical roots, contemporary relevance, and challenges to social justice.

Q2 Arguments (40 marks)

1. Democracy slows down the Pace of Development
2. Women's Empowerment in India is an urban Phenomenon

Q3 Reports: (20 marks)

1. Chenab Rail Bridge
2. India's Forex Reserve

Q4 Precis: one third of its length (15 marks)

The choices we make on a daily basis—wearing a seatbelt, lifting heavy objects correctly or purposely staying out of any dangerous situation—can either ensure our safety or bring about potentially harmful circumstances.

You and I need to make a decision that we are going to get our lives in order. Exercising self-control, self-discipline and establishing boundaries and borders in our lives are some of the most important things we can do. A life without discipline is one that's filled with carelessness.

We can think it's kind of exciting to live life on the edge. We like the image of "Yeah! That's me! Living on the edge! Woo-hoo!" It's become a popular way to look at life. But if you see, even highways have lines, which provide margins for our safety while we're driving. If we go over one side, we'll go into the ditch. If we cross over the line in the middle, we could get killed. And we like those lines because they help to keep us safe. Sometimes we don't even realize how lines help to keep us safe.

I'm not proud of this, but for the first 20 years of my life at work, I ignored my limits. I felt horrible, physically, most of the time. I used to tell myself, "I know I have limits and that I've reached them, but I'm going to ignore them and see if or how long I can get by with it." I ran to doctors, trying to make myself feel better through pills, vitamins, natural stuff and anything I could get my hands on. Some of the doctors would tell me, "It's just stress." That just made me mad. I thought stress meant you don't like what you do or can't handle life, and I love what I do. But I kept pushing myself, travelling, doing speaking engagements and so on— simply exhausting myself.

Finally, I understood I was living an unsustainable life and needed to make some changes in my outlook and lifestyle.

You and I don't have to be like everyone else or keep up with anyone else. Each of us needs to be exactly the way we are, and we don't have to apologize for it. We're not all alike, and we need to find a comfort zone in which we can enjoy our lives instead of making ourselves sick with an overload of stress and pressure.

Q5 Comprehension: (20 marks)

Read the passage given below:

1 In spite of all the honours that we heaped upon him, Pasteur, as has been said, remained simple at heart. Perhaps the imagery of his boyhood days, when he drew the familiar scenes of his birthplace, and the longing to be a great artist, never wholly left him. In truth he did become a great artist, though after his sixteenth year he abandoned the brush forever. Like every artist of worth, he put his whole soul and energy into his work, and it was this very energy that in the end wore him out. For him, each sufferer was something more than just a case that was to be cured. He looked upon the fight against hydrophobia as a battle, and he was absorbed in his determination to win. The sight of injured children, particularly, moved him to an indescribable extent. He suffered with his patients, and yet he would not deny himself a share in that suffering. His greatest grief was when sheer physical exhaustion made him give up his active work. He retired to the estate at Villeneuve Etang, where he had his kennels for the study of rabies, and there he passed his last summer, as his great biographer, Vallery Radot, has said, "practising the Gospel virtues."

2 "He revered the faith of his fathers, "says the same writer, "and wished without ostentation or mystery to receive its aid during his last period."

3 The attitude of this man to the science he had done so much to perfect can be best summed up in a sentence that he is reputed once to have uttered, concerning the materialism of many of his contemporaries in similar branches of learning to his own: "The more I contemplate the mysteries of Nature, the more my faith becomes like that of a peasant."

4 But even then in retirement he loved to see his former pupils, and it was then he would reiterate his life principles: "Work, " he would say, "never cease to work." So well had he kept this precept that he began rapidly to sink from exhaustion.

5 Finally on September 27, 1895, when someone leant over his bed to offer him a cup of milk, he said sadly: "I cannot, " and with a look of perfect resignation and peace, seemed to fall asleep. He never again opened his eyes to the cares and sufferings of a world, which he had done so much to relieve and to conquer. He was within three months of his seventy-third birthday.

6 Thus passed, as simply as a child, the man whom the French people were to vote for at a plebiscite as the greatest man that France had ever produced. Napoleon, who has always been considered the idol of France, was placed fifth.

7 No greater tribute could have been paid to Louis Pasteur, the tanner's son, the scientist, the man of peace, the patient worker for humanity.

Answer the following questions:

a. Even accolades and honours did not change the simple man that Pasteur was. Why?

b. How did Pasteur engage himself in the estate?

c What advice did he always give to his pupils?

d How did France, the country of his birth, honour this great scientist?

e Find the words from the passage which mean the same as:

    1.People belonging to the same period

    2. Vote by the people of the country to decide a matter of national importance

Q6 below given are sentences with highlighted phrases. You are required to choose the best substitute for the given options.

a I don't mind talking to him about the project but he is <u>a person who thinks only of himself.</u>

1. Eccentric
2. Boaster
3. Egoist
4. Proud

b She <u>makes it certain</u> that she will never fight with her best friend over a pity thing like this.

1. Assures
2. Insures
3. Ensures
4. Seizures

c We visited the ancient palace yesterday, there we saw old manuscripts written by saints, we tried but <u>it was not clear enough to be read.</u>

1. Corrigible
2. Legible
3. Negligible
4. Illegible

d This is his first press conference with the media, he is anxious because he <u>speaks less</u>.

1. Sullen
2. Terse
3. Garrulous
4. Reticent

e My brother is a theatre artist who performs and <u>expresses stories or thoughts through gestures.</u>

1. Pantomime
2. Mimic
3. Depictions
4. Ham

Q7 Do as directed (10 marks)

1. We saw small bits of grass peeping through the small cracks. (Rewrite using Present Perfect Continuous Tense)

2. We saw a tree bare of all leaves in the cold winter months. (Frame a Wh-question to get the underline part as an answer)

3. A rainbow colours the entire sky. (Begin the sentence with "The entire sky……."/Change the voice)

4. We went to a rocky beach. (Add a question tag)

5. Nature soothes and nurtures. (Use 'not only….but also')

6. We have a hibiscus plant in our garden. (Frame a Wh-question to get the underline part as an answer)

7. Clouds take new shapes with every passing moment. (Rewrite using Present Continuous Tense)

8. The flower comes to life only for a day. (Identify the tense)

9. Innumerable stars shine across the infinite sky. (Rewrite using modal auxiliary verb showing 'possibility')

10. Our problems are so colossal. (Make it exclamatory)

Q8 Fill in the blanks with suitable determiners.

(i)……………. books are missing from the library. (Any, Some)

(ii) She has not solved…………….. sums, (many, any)

(iii) This book is mine but………………. is yours, (that, any)

(iv) boys have done their work. (That, These)

(v) He didn't make………… progress, (much, many)

Q9 Fill in the blanks with the appropriate form of modals.(5 marks)

1. The villagers………………….. use kerosene lamps a few years ago. (must, had to)

2. The old lady…………… take a bath every day before taking meals, (ought to, should)

3. She……………….. finish this work before I go. (has to, must)

4. Ramesh said that they…………….. report for duty on Monday, (should, ought to)

5. We………………………….. prepare our lessons well before the examination. (ought to, must)

6.

Q1 Essay : write any 4 (80 marks)

A. Mental Health Awareness and Support in India

B. India's Role in the Global Economy

C. Corruption in Indian Politics: Causes and Solutions

D. The Role of Foreign Direct Investment (FDI) in India's Economic Development

E. The Role of Media in Bridging Social Inequality

F. Promoting Innovation and Startups in India

Q2 Arguments (40 marks)

1. India's Healthcare System is Ill-Prepared to Handle Pandemics."

2. India's Space Program is a Misallocation of Resources

Q3 Reports: (20 marks)

1. Universal Healthcare in India

2. Vocational Education in India

Q4 Precis: one third of its length (15 marks)

My sister, Mrs. Joe Gargery, was more than twenty years older than I, and had established a great reputation with herself and the neighbours because she had brought me up "by hand." Having at that time to find out for myself what the expression meant, and knowing her to have a hard and heavy hand, and to be much in the habit of laying it upon her husband as well as upon me, I supposed that Joe Gargery and I were both brought up by hand.

She was not a good-looking woman, my sister; and I had a general impression that she must have made Joe Gargery marry her by hand. Joe was a fair man, with curls of flaxen hair on each side of his smooth face, and with eyes of such a very undecided blue that they seemed to have somehow got mixed with their own whites. He was a mild, good-natured, sweet-tempered, easy-going, foolish, dear fellow,—a sort of Hercules in strength, and also in weakness.

My sister, Mrs. Joe, with black hair and eyes, had such a prevailing redness of skin that I sometimes used to wonder whether it was possible she washed herself with a nutmeg-grater instead of soap. She was tall and bony, and almost always wore a coarse apron, fastened over her figure behind with two loops, and having a square impregnable bib in front, that was stuck full of pins and needles. She made it a powerful merit in herself, and a strong reproach against Joe, that she wore this apron so much. Though I really see no reason why she should have worn it at all; or why, if she did wear it at all, she should not have taken it off, every day of her life.

Joe's forge adjoined our house, which was a wooden house, as many of the dwellings in our country were,—most of them, at that time. When I ran home from the churchyard, the forge was shut up, and Joe was sitting alone in the kitchen.

Q5 Comprehension: (20 marks)

Read the passage given below:

1. Too many parents these days can't say no. As a result, they find themselves raising 'children' who respond greedily to the advertisements aimed right at them. Even getting what they want doesn't satisfy some kids; they only want more. Now, a growing number of psychologists, educators and parents think it's time to stop the madness and start teaching kids about what's really important: values like hard work, contentment, honesty and compassion. The struggle to set limits has never been tougherand the stakes have never been higher. One recent study of adults who were overindulged as children, paints a discouraging picture of their future: when given too much too soon, they grow up to be adults who have difficulty coping with life's disappointments. They also have a distorted sense of entitlement that gets in the way of success in the workplace and in relationships.

2. Psychologists say that parents who overindulge their kids, set them up to be more vulnerable to future anxiety and depression. Today's parents themselves raised on values of thrift and self service, grew up in a culture where no was a household word. Today's kids want much more, partly because there is so much more to want. The oldest members of this generation were bom in the late 1980s, just as PCs and video games were making their assault on the family room. They think of MP3 players and flat screen TV as essential utilities, and they have developed strategies to get them. One survey of teenagers found that when they crave for something new, most expect to ask nine times before their parents give in. By every measure, parents are shelling

out record amounts. In the heat of this buying blitz, even parents who desperately need to say no find themselves reaching for their credit cards.

3. Today's parents aren't equipped to deal with the problem. Many of them, raised in the 1960s and '70s, swore they'd act differently from their parents and have closer relationships with their own children. Many even wear the same designer clothes as their kids and listen to the same music. And they work more hours; at the end of a long week, it's tempting to buy peace with 'yes' and not mar precious family time with conflict. Anxiety about the future is another factor. How do well intentioned parents say no to all the sports gear and arts and language lessons they believe will help their kids thrive in an increasingly competitive world? Experts agree : too much love won't spoil a child. Too few limits will.

4. What parents need to find is a balance between the advantages of an affluent society and the critical life lessons that come from waiting, saving and working hard to achieve goals. That search for balance has to start early. Children need limits on their behaviour because they feel better and more secure when they live within a secured structure. Older children learn self control by watching how others, especially parents act. Learning how to overcome challenges is essential to becoming a successful adult. Few parents ask kids to do chores. They think their kids are already overburdened by social and academic pressures. Every individual can be of service to others, and life has meaning beyond one's own immediate happiness. That means parents eager to teach values have to take a long, hard look at their own.

Answer the following:

(i) What values do parents and teachers want children to learn?

(ii) What are the results of giving the children too much too soon?

(iii) What is the balance which the parents need to have in today's world?

(iv) What is the necessity to set limits for children?

v) Pick out words from the passage that mean the same as the following:

    a. a feeling of satisfaction

    b. valuable

    c. important

    d. weak and easy to hurt physically or emotionally

Q6 Do as directed (10 marks)

1. My father was a medical professional. (Add a question tag)
2. My father was a medical professional. (Frame a Wh-question to get the underline part as an answer)
3. My father was a medical professional. (Frame a Wh-question to get the underline part as an answer)
4. They had all become a part and parcel of our existence. (Identify the tense)
5. They had all become a part and parcel of our existence. (Rewrite using 'Simple Past Tense')
6. Our house was in a corner of the campus. (Choose the correct question tag)

    i. was it? ii. wasn't he? iii. wasn't it?

7. The officer's club was adjacent to the boundary wall of our garden. (Frame a Wh-question to get the underline part as an answer)
8. The magnificent trees constantly attracted squirrels. (Begin the sentence with 'Squirrels.......'/Change the voice)
9. The holidays provided an opportunity for me. (Rewrite using 'Present Perfect Continuous Tense')
10. The holidays provided an opportunity for me. (Frame a Wh-question to get the underline part as an answer)

Q7 Fill in the blanks with suitable determiners

1. Ramu is ____ honest man who runs ____ small shop around the corner. (a, a / an, a)
2. Have you seen ____ Taj Mahal? It is one of the seven wonders of the world. (the, a)
3. Are ____ your books? Can you share them with me? (these/this)
4. Do you have ____ buns left? I need to buy ____. (any/few, some/several)
5. ____ of the students got ____ chocolates from the teacher. (each, some / each, any)

Q8 Fill in the blanks with appropriate prepositions using the given alternatives.

1. The lion was killed…………………… the hunter……………………… a sword, (in, on, by, with)
2. Father divided his property……………………… four sons, (between, among, of, in)
3. He has been living in this house…………………….. 1985. (for, since, in, on)
4. I shall return………………… a month, (in, of, on, for)
5. The Ramayana is lying………………… the table, (in, of, on, for)

Q9 Fill in the blanks with the correct modals

1. You ___ be punctual. (should/ought)
2. One __ repay all their debts. (must/ought to)
3. __ you show me the road to the market? (could/might)
4. The child __ be taken to hospital immediately. (must/might)
5. ___ you have hot chocolate? (shall/will)

7.

Q1 Essay : write any 4 (80 marks)

A. The implementation of the Citizenship Amendment Act (CAA) will have positive effects on India's refugee policy.

B. Insurgency in Jammu and Kashmir: historical context and current challenges

C. Environmental ethics in Indian philosophy

D. The role of India and China in global governance

E. Role of artificial intelligence in governance

F. Censorship is necessary to protect the society from harmful ideas

Q2 Arguments (40 marks)

1. The death penalty should be abolished in India
2. India's healthcare system needs more privatisation to improve efficiency and accessibility

Q3 Reports: (20 marks)

1. Bharat's MSME Boom
2. International Space Station

Q4 Precis: one third of its length (15 marks)

Reading is a fundamental skill that plays a vital role in our lives. It's not just about deciphering words on a page but about the doors it opens, the knowledge it imparts, and the worlds it allows us to explore. Reading is an essential tool for learning, expanding our horizons, and fostering imagination.

When we read, we acquire knowledge. Whether it's reading textbooks, newspapers, or online articles, we gain information that helps us understand the world. Books, in particular, are a treasure trove of knowledge. They contain the wisdom of generations, the discoveries of great minds, and the stories of diverse cultures. Reading books can educate us on history, science, literature, and countless other subjects. It's like having a mentor, guiding us through the complexities of life.

Reading also broadens our horizons. It exposes us to different viewpoints, perspectives, and experiences. When we read about characters from various backgrounds or explore far-off lands through the pages of a novel, we step into their shoes and see the world from a different angle. This broadening of perspective fosters empathy and understanding, making us more tolerant and open-minded individuals.

Q5 Comprehension: (20 marks)

Read the passage given below:

Can you imagine a college without walls, professors or classrooms? Educator Bunker Roy can. More than 40 years ago, Roy, now 69, founded the Barefoot College in Tilonia, Rajasthan. His school admits rural women, often grandmothers and teaches them the basics of solar engineering and freshwater technology. His efforts have yielded enormous benefits. When the women return to their homes, they are trained enough to provide their communities, some of the world's most lonely places, with electricity and clean water. They also gain something important: a newfound self-confidence. The Barefoot model has already been used to empower women throughout Asia, Africa, and Latin America. Last year, former President Bill Clinton presented Roy with a Clinton Global Citizen Award, which honours leaders who are solving the world's problems in effective ways.

2. If you go all over the world, to very remote villages, you will often find only very old people and very young people. The men have already left. So two ideas were put into practice in order to make the Barefoot Model work. First it was declared that men are untrainable, restless, always ready to move, ambitious, and they all want a certificate to show for their efforts. And the moment you give one of them a certificate, he leaves the village looking for a job in the city. That is how, the simple, practical solution of training grandmothers came up. They are sympathetic, tolerant, willing to learn, and patient. All the qualities you need are there. And the second idea was not to give out certificates. Because the moment a certificate is given, a woman, like a man, will see it as a passport for leaving rural areas and going to urban areas to find a job.

3. Barefoot College follows the lifestyle of Mahatma Gandhi: Students eat, sleep, and work on the floor. They can work for 20 years or they can go home the next day. As of today, 604 women solar engineers from 1083 villages in 63 countries have been trained. The engineers have given solar power to 45,000 houses. These were done by women who had never left their homes before. They hate the idea of leaving their

families and getting on a plane. When they reach India, sometimes after 19 hours of travel, they are faced with strange food, strange people, and a strange language. All the training is done in sign language. Yet in six months, they will know more about solar engineering than most university graduates. Some women face problems at home while attending college. Most of the husbands do not like their wives going to these colleges and tell them not to come back if they do so. But, on her return when she is able to help provide her village with solar electricity, her husband wants her to get back home. The respect she now has is enormous and she considers herself no less than solar engineers. Bunker Roy dreams of providing the world's 47 least developed countries with Barefoot College trained grandmothers and solar electrify more than 1,00,000 houses.

Answer the following questions briefly: 5X4=20

a. How is Barefoot College different from other colleges?

b. What did the women gain from the college apart from technology?

c. What are the difficulties the women have to face during their travel and their life in Tilonia, Rajasthan?

d. How do the women consider themselves professionally, after their training?

e. What is the narrator's dream about solar electrification?

Q6 Do as directed (10 marks)

1. It is probable that he will never come back. (Begin: In …)

2. He said to me, 'Where are you going?' (Begin: He asked me …)

3. As soon as the chief guest had arrived the play began. (Begin: No sooner ….)

4. I was surprised at his behaviour. (Begin: His …)

5. He will certainly succeed. (Begin: He is …)

6. He is the best student in the class. (Use better instead of best)

7. He is too weak to stand up without help.

8. He tucked the gun under his arm and rushed towards the bridge. (End: … his arm.)

9. We were late. Consequently, we missed the train. (Rewrite with as or since)

10. Though I had a headache, I enjoyed the movie. (Rewrite with in spite of)

Q7 Make sentences for the following idioms to illustrate their meaning (5)

a. To build a castle in the air
b. To beat around the bush
c. Birds of a feather
d. All's well that ends well
e. Every dark cloud has a silver lining

Q8 Fill in the blanks with the appropriate form of modals.(5 marks)

a. _____ you please keep the noise down? I'm trying to concentrate. (Can / Would / Should)
b. You _____ not park here; it's a no-parking zone. (may / should / must)
c. They _____ finish the project on time; they're working hard. (should / might / will)
d. _____ you please pass the salt? (will / can / could)
e. I _____ help you if I could. (will / would / might)

Q9 Insert a preposition, where necessary

a. He asked his father …………………….. money.
b. They paid me …………………….. the books.
c. I thought he would offer Ann the job, but he offered it …………………….. me.
d. Keep me a place, and keep a place …………………….. Ann too.
e. They showed us photographs …………………….. their baby.

8.

Q1 Essay : write any 4 (80 marks)

A. The implementation of the Citizenship Amendment Act (CAA) will have positive effects on India's refugee policy.

B. Insurgency in Jammu and Kashmir: historical context and current challenges

C. Environmental ethics in Indian philosophy

D. The role of India and China in global governance

E. Role of artificial intelligence in governance

F. Censorship is necessary to protect the society from harmful ideas

Q2 Arguments (40 marks)

1. The death penalty should be abolished in India
2. India's healthcare system needs more privatisation to improve efficiency and accessibility

Q3 Reports: (20 marks)

1. Bharat's MSME Boom
2. International Space Station

Q4 Precis: one third of its length (15 marks)

Reading is a fundamental skill that plays a vital role in our lives. It's not just about deciphering words on a page but about the doors it opens, the knowledge it imparts, and the worlds it allows us to explore. Reading is an essential tool for learning, expanding our horizons, and fostering imagination.

When we read, we acquire knowledge. Whether it's reading textbooks, newspapers, or online articles, we gain information that helps us understand the world. Books, in particular, are a treasure trove of knowledge. They contain the wisdom of generations, the discoveries of great minds, and the stories of diverse cultures. Reading books can educate us on history, science, literature, and countless other subjects. It's like having a mentor, guiding us through the complexities of life.

Reading also broadens our horizons. It exposes us to different viewpoints, perspectives, and experiences. When we read about characters from various backgrounds or explore far-off lands through the pages of a novel, we step into their shoes and see the world from a different angle. This broadening of perspective fosters empathy and understanding, making us more tolerant and open-minded individuals.

Q5 Comprehension: (20 marks)

Read the passage given below:

Can you imagine a college without walls, professors or classrooms? Educator Bunker Roy can. More than 40 years ago, Roy, now 69, founded the Barefoot College in Tilonia, Rajasthan. His school admits rural women, often grandmothers and teaches them the basics of solar engineering and freshwater technology. His efforts have yielded enormous benefits. When the women return to their homes, they are trained enough to provide their communities, some of the world's most lonely places, with electricity and clean water. They also gain something important: a newfound self-confidence. The Barefoot model has already been used to empower women throughout Asia, Africa, and Latin America. Last year, former President Bill Clinton presented Roy with a Clinton Global Citizen Award, which honours leaders who are solving the world's problems in effective ways.

2. If you go all over the world, to very remote villages, you will often find only very old people and very young people. The men have already left. So two ideas were put into practice in order to make the Barefoot Model work. First it was declared that men are untrainable, restless, always ready to move, ambitious, and they all want a certificate to show for their efforts. And the moment you give one of them a certificate, he leaves the village looking for a job in the city. That is how, the simple, practical solution of training grandmothers came up. They are sympathetic, tolerant, willing to learn, and patient. All the qualities you need are there. And the second idea was not to give out certificates. Because the moment a certificate is given, a woman, like a man, will see it as a passport for leaving rural areas and going to urban areas to find a job.

3. Barefoot College follows the lifestyle of Mahatma Gandhi: Students eat, sleep, and work on the floor. They can work for 20 years or they can go home the next day. As of today, 604 women solar engineers from 1083 villages in 63 countries have been trained. The engineers have given solar power to 45,000 houses. These were done by women who had never left their homes before. They hate the idea of leaving their

families and getting on a plane. When they reach India, sometimes after 19 hours of travel, they are faced with strange food, strange people, and a strange language. All the training is done in sign language. Yet in six months, they will know more about solar engineering than most university graduates. Some women face problems at home while attending college. Most of the husbands do not like their wives going to these colleges and tell them not to come back if they do so. But, on her return when she is able to help provide her village with solar electricity, her husband wants her to get back home. The respect she now has is enormous and she considers herself no less than solar engineers. Bunker Roy dreams of providing the world's 47 least developed countries with Barefoot College trained grandmothers and solar electrify more than 1,00,000 houses.

Answer the following questions briefly: 5X4=20

a. How is Barefoot College different from other colleges?

b. What did the women gain from the college apart from technology?

c. What are the difficulties the women have to face during their travel and their life in Tilonia, Rajasthan?

d. How do the women consider themselves professionally, after their training?

e. What is the narrator's dream about solar electrification?

Q6 Do as directed (10 marks)

1. It is probable that he will never come back. (Begin: In …)

2. He said to me, 'Where are you going?' (Begin: He asked me …)

3. As soon as the chief guest had arrived the play began. (Begin: No sooner ….)

4. I was surprised at his behaviour. (Begin: His …)

5. He will certainly succeed. (Begin: He is …)

6. He is the best student in the class. (Use better instead of best)

7. He is too weak to stand up without help.

8. He tucked the gun under his arm and rushed towards the bridge. (End: … his arm.)

9. We were late. Consequently, we missed the train. (Rewrite with as or since)

10. Though I had a headache, I enjoyed the movie. (Rewrite with in spite of)

Q7 Make sentences for the following idioms to illustrate their meaning (5)

a. To build a castle in the air

b. To beat around the bush

c. Birds of a feather

d. All's well that ends well

e. Every dark cloud has a silver lining

Q8 Fill in the blanks with the appropriate form of modals.(5 marks)

a. _____ you please keep the noise down? I'm trying to concentrate. (Can / Would / Should)

b. You _____ not park here; it's a no-parking zone. (may / should / must)

c. They _____ finish the project on time; they're working hard. (should / might / will)

d. _____ you please pass the salt? (will / can / could)

e. I _____ help you if I could. (will / would / might)

Q9 Insert a preposition, where necessary

a. He asked his father .... money.

b. They paid me .... the books.

c. I thought he would offer Ann the job, but he offered it .... me.

d. Keep me a place, and keep a place .... Ann too.

e. They showed us photographs .... their baby.

9.

Q1 Essay: (any 4) (4x20)

1. Increasing representation and not appeasement can help the cause of women empowerment
2. the ethical implications of genetic engineering and its potential effects on future generations.
3. Challenges and Strategies: Safeguarding India's Internal Security in the 21st Century.
4. The Role of the Indian Judiciary in Upholding Justice and its Impact on Democracy.
5. Is India ready for cashless economy
6. AI and the Enigma of Human Consciousness

Q2 Arguments topic: (2x20)

1. Artificial intelligence will adversely impact the job market.
2. The benefits of nuclear energy outweigh the potential risks and environmental concerns.

Q3 Report topics: (2x10)

1. Evolution of renewable energy technologies
2. Implementation of 5G technology

Q4 Precis (15)

Business cycles are dated according to when the direction of economic activity changes. The peak of the cycle refers to the last month before several key economic indicators—such as employment, output, and retail sales— begin to fall. The trough of the cycle refers to the last month before the same economic indicators begin to rise. Because key economic indicators often change direction at slightly different times, the dating of peaks and troughs is necessarily somewhat subjective. The National Bureau of Economic Research (NBER) is an independent research institution that dates the peaks and troughs of U.S. business cycles. Recent research has shown that the NBER's reference dates for the period before World War I are not truly comparable with those for the modern era because they were determined using different methods and data. In many ways, the term "business cycle" is misleading. "Cycle" seems to imply that there is some regularity in the timing and duration of upswings and downswings in economic activity. The combination of expansions and recessions, the ebb and flow of economic activity, is called the business cycle. For describing the swings in economic activity, therefore, many modern economists prefer the term "short-run economic fluctuations" to "business cycle."

Q5 Reading comprehension (5x4)

Read the passage given below and answer the questions that follow:

1. Today's woman is a highly self-directed person, alive to the sense of her dignity and the importance of her functions in the private domestic domain and the public domain of the world of work. Women are rational in approach, careful in handling situations and want to do things as best as possible. The Fourth World Conference of Women held in Beijing in September 1995 had emphasized that no enduring solution of society's most threatening social, economic and political problems could be found without the participation and empowerment of the women. The 1995 World Summit for Social Development had also emphasised the pivotal role of women in eradicating poverty and mending the social fabric.

2. The Constitution of India had conferred on women equal rights and opportunities political, social, educational and of employment with men. Because of oppressive traditions, superstitions, exploitation and corruption, a majority of women are not allowed to enjoy the rights and opportunities, bestowed on them. One of the major reasons for this state of affairs is the lack of literacy and awareness among women. Education is the main instrument through which we can narrow down the prevailing inequality and accelerate the process of economic and political change in the status of women.

3. The role of women in a society is very important. Women's education is the key to a better life in the future. A recent World Bank study says that educating girls is not a charity, it is good economics and if developing nations are to eradicate poverty, they must educate the girls. The report says that the economic and social returns on investment in education of the girls considerably affect the human development index of the nation. Society would progress only if the status of women is respected and the

presence of an educated woman in the family would ensure education of the family itself. Education and empowerment of women are closely related.

4. Women's education has not received due care and attention from the planners and policymakers. The National Commission for Women has rightly pointed out that even after 50 years of independence, women continue to be treated as the single largest group of backward citizens of India. The role of women in overall development has not been fully understood nor has it been given its full weight in the struggle to eliminate poverty, hunger, injustice and inequality at the national level. Even when we are at the threshold of the 21st century, our society still discriminates against women in matters of their rights and privileges and prevents them from participating in the process of national and societal progress. Various Committees and Commissions have been constituted before and after the independence to evaluate the progress in women's education and to suggest ways and means to enhance the status of women. The female literacy rate has gone up in the 20th century from 0.6 per cent in 1901 to 39.29 per cent in 1991 but India still possesses the largest number of illiterate women in the world. The female literacy index for the year 1991 shows that there are eight States which fall below the national average. The most populous States of the country, UP, MP, Bihar and Rajasthan fall in the category of most backward States as far as female literacy is concerned.

5. The prevailing cultural norms of gender behaviour and the perceived domestic and reproductive roles of women tend to affect the education of girls. Negative attitude towards sending girls to schools, restrictions on their mobility, early marriage, poverty and illiteracy of parents affect the girl's participation in education.

6. Women's political empowerment got a big boost with the Panchayati Raj Act of 1993 which gave them 30 per cent reservation in Village Panchayats, Block Samities and Zila Parishads throughout the country. The National Commission for Women was also set up in 1992 to act as a lobby for women's issues.

7. The educational system is the only institution which can counteract the deep foundations of inequality of sexes that are built in the minds of people through the socialization process. Education is the most important instrument of human resource development. Educational system should be used to revolutionize the traditional attitudes and inculcate new values of equality.

I) Mention any two attributes of a modern woman.

(ii) Why are women's participation and empowerment considered necessary?

(iii) Which factors adversely affect the education of girls?

(iv) What benefits did the women get with the enactment of the Panchayati Raj Act of 1993?

(v) By what process can we remove the sense of inequality of sexes from the minds of the people?

Q6 do as directed (5)

1. I took him around with me . (Change the voice)
2. When I saw the prizes and read the citation Chaitanya had received, I was stupefied. (Use 'No sooner......than')
3. The bird was spotted in pairs almost everyday. (Change the voice)
4. "They have promised that the funds that we have given to initiate the process will be returned to us," Mr. Pawar said. (Rewrite as Indirect Speech)
5. His father would undoubtedly be left shaking his head and burying himself deeper into his newspaper. (Use 'not only...but also')

Q7 Fill with the correct auxiliary verbs (5)

(i) He went there so that he …….. borrow money.

(ii) ……… you please help my son ?

(iii) I …… not go outside now.

(iv) Make haste lest you ……… get late.

(v) My friend did not help me though he ……… have helped.

Q8 Correct the sentences (5)

1. Rahul went to school despite of having a fever.
2. I haven't seen Susan since six years.
3. Lisa is busy at the work, so she can't make it on time.

4. Our mathematics teacher is giving us too much tasks.

5. Do not advice her, she won't listen.

Q9 Choose the appropriate preposition to complete the sentence:(5)

1. I'll meet you ……………….. the evening.

2. I'll call you ……………….. eight o'clock.

3. We walked ……………….. the edge of the forest.

4. Immediately ……………….. passing his exams he is going to visit his grandparents.

5. Mohan has been missing ……………….. last month.

Q10 Fill in the blanks with appropriate determiners (5)

1. Ramu is ____ honest man who runs ____ small shop around the corner.

2. Have you seen ____ Taj Mahal? It is one of the seven wonders of the world.

3. Are ____ your books? Can you share them with me?

4. Do you have ____ buns left? I need to buy ____.

5. ____ of the students got ____ chocolates from the teacher.

www.ingramcontent.com/pod-product-compliance
Lightning Source LLC
LaVergne TN
LVHW070526070526
838199LV00073B/6711